MOON 12
C. 1

LINCOLN CHRISTIAN UNIVERSITY

new hope
twelve talks by
Sun Myung Moon

 P9-DFS-126

Published by

THE HOLY SPIRIT ASSOCIATION
FOR THE UNIFICATION OF WORLD CHRISTIANITY, INC.

© Copyright, 1973, by The Holy Spirit Association for the Unification of World Christianit.

All rights reserved. Except for the inclusion of brief quotations in a review, no part of this book may be reproduced or utilized in any form or by any means, electronic or mechanical, including photocopying, recording or by any information storage and retrieval system, without permission in writing from the publisher.

Library of Congress Catalog Number 73-88416

Printed in the United States of America

HSA-UWC, Inc.
1365 Connecticut Avenue, N. W.
Washington, D. C.   20036

To restore the world
let us go forth with the Father's heart
in the shoes of a servant,
shedding tears for man,
sweat for the earth,
and blood for heaven.

Preface

On Easter morning in 1936, Sun Myung Moon was deep in prayer on a Korean mountainside when Jesus Christ appeared to him and told him that he had an important mission to accomplish in the fulfillment of God's providence. He was then sixteen years old. For the next nine years, Sun Myung Moon studied intensely and struggled to prepare himself for his responsibility. In those years of prayer, he discovered a series of principles through which it was possible to clearly understand the spiritual and physical nature of the universe, the process and meaning of history, as well as the inner meanings to the parables and symbols of the Bible and the purpose of all religions.

After the end of World War II Korea was liberated from Japanese occupation, and forty years of religious persecution ended. Rev. Moon then began his public ministry, making known to Christians the deep truths which had been revealed to him. Only a few precious months later, however, Korea was partitioned into north and south, and Communist forces swept into the north, where Rev. Moon was at that time teaching. Suppression of religion, especially Christianity, by the Korean Communists far surpassed even what had been experienced under the Japanese. Christians were expected to conform to the new atheistic society in word and action.

Sun Myung Moon had already gained quite a large following as a Christian leader in Pyungyang, and he soon came to the attention of the Communist authorities. One night without warning, he was taken to the Dae Dong Police Department and was tortured and brutally beaten until he was left for dead in the prison yard. There he was found by his congregation. He soon revived and began to preach again.

Accordingly, Rev. Moon was soon after rearrested and sent to a labor camp further north, at Hung-nam. When he entered the camp, he immediately knew he had been sent there to die. The prisoners were deliberately overworked and underfed, and they were forced to work long hours mining lime, sometimes with their bare hands, and loading heavy bags for shipment. Usually men did not survive life in that camp for more than six months, but Sun Myung Moon realized the importance of the message he had to give the world, and he was determined that he would endure all difficulties until the day when he was free again to continue his work. Although the prisoners' work quotas were purposely set higher than it was possible for them to attain, Rev. Moon made up his mind to surpass them. He lived in the labor camp for two years and ten months, and he was even given an award for his outstanding work record.

We know very little of his life at Hung-nam from his own words, but Rev. Moon's early followers tell us that the other prisoners seldom saw him sleep. When everyone went to sleep at night, he was already in prayer, and when they awakened the next morning, they saw him praying again.

He has said that during that time, he could never pray to God in the ordinary way:

> I never prayed from weakness. I never complained. I was never angry at my situation. I never even asked His help, but was always busy comforting Him and telling Him not to worry about me. The Father knows me so well. He already knew my suffering. How could I tell Him about my suffering and cause His heart to grieve still more? I could only tell Him that I would never be defeated by my suffering.

Although in prison Rev. Moon could never speak about the Divine Principle, other prisoners were attracted to him by his life as a man of God. Many men had dreams or visions which led them to seek him out. Even in that prison situation Sun Myung Moon found those who had been prepared by God for this time in history. It is from those men that we have learned the story of his life in the labor camp.

In June 1950 when the Korean war broke out, American B-29's bombed the industrial area around Hung-nam prison. As the United Nations landing party advanced from the sea, the prison authorities began to execute all prisoners. The day before it was Sun Myung Moon's turn to be shot, a naval gun bombardment by the UN forces began at Hung-nam. Under such fire, the Communist authorities fled the area, and he along with the other prisoners was freed by the United Nations forces on October 14, 1950.

The stream of refugees had begun their flight to South Korea, but the roads were impassable because of military operations. Therefore, the thousands of people struggled their way south walking over the mountain trails. Rev. Moon's former followers in Pyungyang had been scattered. He walked the hundred miles back to the city and tried to locate each one. One of his fellow prisoners had followed him from Hung-nam, but this man's leg was broken, and he could not walk the long miles to the south. Rev. Moon carried this man on his back on a bicycle the six hundred miles to Pusan. There again they began to give the message of new hope.

In 1954 Rev. Moon formally began the Unification Church (The Holy Spirit Association for the Unification of World Christianity) in Korea. There are now headquarters in more than forty countries and centers in more than 120 cities in the United States.

The Unification Church is formed around the Divine Principle, a set of principles based on the patterns which Rev. Moon found in the Bible during his years of search. He discovered that God has been using a consistent strategy to save man – through the Old Testament and the New – that provides the foundation for Jesus' life and teachings. In the light of the principles of creation and restoration which God is still using in the world today, Christians can find new insight into the puzzling problems of faith and Bible interpretation – but even more, they will find deeper meaning in the daily leading of their lives.

Visitors to the Unification Church's residential communities often remark on the wide variety of background, personality, and even age of the members who are nevertheless so obviously united in heart. Around the world, people of all ages can be found working together as one family of Christians – transcendent of barriers of culture and even longstanding national enmities – living with the purpose of bringing the reality of God and His love to the people of the world.

We live today in a time of fundamental confusion. It is not, however, an outward confusion alone, but also a crisis in our faith. Christianity *is* in crisis. But this can also become a time of new hope, because we are being called to come to terms with the most fundamental questions of all.

We have lost control of our food production, of the ethics of our government, and even of our earth's oxygen supply. We expect that science will in due course solve these problems of our physical environment, however uncomfortable we may be in the meantime. But where can we turn to solve the problems of faith and morality? We must also regain control of our spiritual and moral life, where confusion causes the greatest suffering and has the most profound consequences. Our Christianity must go deep enough to offer the world practical solutions to moral questions: Where is the balance between the immorality of killing individual human beings in war, and the immorality of abandoning whole nations to the domination of an alien power? How can we reconcile "the new morality" with our intuitive feelings about Christian morality? Why is it, after all, that the family and marriage should be sacred? Is there finally anything eternal – and therefore absolute – in human nature and life?

Bare speculations whether or not God exists are less meaningful to us than the question, "If God exists, why doesn't He do something about the world?" Christians must be able to answer that question. Finding new hope in today's world is not an easy matter. People are no longer satisfied with ephemeral ideals, but to be reinspired we must be able to say clearly: What is good and evil in real life? In exactly what way has God been working in history? What is God and how can we know Him ultimately? And what does God expect of Christians in this age of despair?

Only a Christian message that can deal with ultimate questions – and provide clear and simple answers – can bring new hope today. Rev. Sun Myung Moon comes bringing such a message.

Editor's Note

The talks in this book have been compiled from among the many speeches given by Sun Myung Moon in 1971, 1972, and 1973 to members at Unification Church residential and training Centers in the United States and Canada.

The editor has worked with transcripts of simultaneous translations from the Korean of Rev. Moon's talks. Translation was done by Mrs. Won Pok Choi or Mr. Young Whi Kim. The rendering of any Oriental language into English presents many difficulties to the translator, particularly when he has to deal with abstract ideas and terminology. In this case, the translators had the additional problem of producing immediately a concise verbal account in English. Despite these difficulties, Rev. Moon's talks passed through their interpreters retaining their abundant inspiration, challenge and beauty.

Since Rev. Moon addressed his talks to members of the Unification Church, he often used terminology which is familiar to them through their study of the Divine Principle. For a complete explanation of terms and concepts which may be unfamiliar to the reader, we recommend your reference to *The Divine Principle*, which may be obtained from the publisher.

With confidence that you will find in these chapters a new hope for the realization of the fullness of life with God in an ideal world, we are happy to offer this book.

Washington, D. C.   Rebecca Salonen
October 1, 1973

ix

Contents

PREFACE / *v*

EDITOR'S NOTE / *ix*

FAITH AND REALITY / *1*

THE BASIS OF GOOD AND EVIL / *11*

MAY GOD PROTECT US / *23*

THREE STAGES OF JUDGMENT / *31*

THE FORMULA FOR GOD'S PROVIDENCE / *43*

HEART / *51*

AMERICA IN GOD'S PROVIDENCE / *59*

CHILDREN OF THE HEAVENLY FATHER / *67*

GOD'S TRUE NATION / *75*

CHALLENGE AND VICTORY / *81*

WAY OF LIFE / *87*

GOD'S GRIEF / *95*

Faith and Reality

The life of faith does not depend on the concrete, visible reality of this physical world, but has to do with the invisible God. We are living in a world of practical reality, so we have to deal with practical issues on this earth. However, the life of faith belongs to another realm, and we cannot apply the same standards or deal with the same issues.

In this world we all seek happiness and joy. We as individual beings can never find happiness, but we need some other element with which to bring it about – another person, material things, an intellectual goal. We can apply certain criteria to everything in the world. Unless we are finding other things or people that stimulate us and make us happy, we cannot make progress in life. In other words, we find happiness through something objective which stimulates us. In our academic life, we are happy as we pursue intellectual reality. But happiness comes over a period of time as we strive to reach a high goal or ideal. The problem always is, "How can I establish a relationship between myself and my object that will bring happiness?"

Unhappiness, depression and despair will be produced whenever we fail to maintain the proper relationship with our object. In order for us to continue living it is absolutely necessary to have a continuous and positive objective stimulus. All the elements of success and failure develop around this relationship. How are you going to continue to be positively stimulated in your academic work? That is the key to success. Although you may set up many ideal standards in the world of reality, if this continuous stimulus is cut off, you will fail to reach the goal.

The same principle applies also to the life of faith. But when I talk about the life of faith we experience in this world, there sometimes seems to us to be no evidence or scientific method to validate our faith. We are dealing with invisible and often impractical things to which we cannot apply the same kind of cognition as in the world of reality. The problem therefore is, how can we find and relate concretely to a source of positive stimulus in our life of faith? How can we be happy in our life of faith?

Whenever the problem of the physical life of human beings comes up, we meet questions concerning material or substantial things. But in the world of faith, there is the problem of cognition, or the question of knowledge. Thus, the realm of consciousness – faith or reality – becomes very important. How can we make a connection between the life of faith and the life of this world through our knowledge? When we think only of the lives of other people, it is difficult to discover this stimulus. But there is no other way to set up a standard for ourselves but by observing and studying all of the central figures in God's providence from Adam on. We have to study closely how these people, God's dispensational figures, including the past saints and sages, lived in their interaction with human beings, and how they related to material things. Let us look at Noah, Abraham, Moses, John the Baptist, and other dispensational figures. We must be curious about their objectives and motives. This will be the issue.

All of these great men started their life of faith centered not on themselves, but on God. Why do we have to respect and sometimes even worship them? Simply because they were guided by God, not by themselves. Also, we should know what kind of life they lived for God in their age. We find that they all had a conflict – their life of faith versus the life of reality. We find further that they were not of one will when they faced these conflicts, but that they solved the problem when they brought themselves to center on God, not on their own desires. And we know that because of this conflict between God's side and the world's side, these people endured persecution and suffering. That is why they are great people.

Always we find that their life in this world was lonely because they suffered so much and were rejected by the world. They usually had no one to convey their thoughts and feelings to; they could go only to God. And when we look at their lives in the world, their material lives, we find that they were so limited in their material life that they naturally turned their hearts and lives toward God. When we imagine the consciousness they must have had, we can see that the scope of their thinking was narrowed down so that they saw everything centered on God. That was their life. They had to live their lives centering on oneness with God.

In every area – relationships with people, knowledge, material things –

they plunged themselves into a relationship with God, because there was no one else to rely on except God. There was no way to have give and take horizontally, to seek an object of happiness in their surroundings, so they concentrated on finding their object in God – more seriously than they had sought an object in this world. Because the foundation for their faith was so narrow, they had to rely on heaven to get through such a narrow channel to God. And thus they opened new realms by embracing God with hope and the desire for a higher ideal.

Even if only a narrow way was open to God, they were not discouraged. We should also be optimistic in the same situation. There is always a way to continue. We cannot be discontented. God created all things for the happiness and satisfaction and contentment of people. So even when we reach this narrow pass, we will not feel defeated, because from that narrow point a new relationship between ourselves and God will open up. There we will find true happiness and greater contentment. For example, Saint Francis emphasized pure poverty, a nothingness in which he could find happiness, appreciation and satisfaction. From that point on, God could work with him and let him feel happy and joyful. Oneness with God could be created from that point.

We have to realize that we as fallen people are standing in between two lines representing God's side and the world's side. We have to recognize the narrowing down of those lines; then we will know when the new era of happiness and joy will begin. You know the life of Noah. When he met a deadlock – one hundred twenty years of receiving persecution while he built his ark – at that point he was forced into a narrow position, and a new life of faith began. You will have created a new realm of happiness and blessing when you are able to overcome the point of being narrowed down, when you prove you can open a new door to your relationship with God.

For years Noah could only think of building the ark, and went to the mountain to work there. Do you think there is a woman who can endure ten years with such a husband? An American wife sues for a divorce if her husband goes away for six months. Noah's work was not an ordinary task. Therefore this event must have been the greatest event after God created man. And if a wife starts to persecute her husband, the children will also do the same with her. How much pain Noah must have felt in his heart when his family could not understand him. Because of this he had great troubles. When he asked his family to get him something to eat, or something to wear, they treated him as if he were a beggar. Noah could stand the persecutions outside of his family – from the village or from the nation. But these sufferings and persecutions were coming from inside his own family, the most difficult for him to bear. In spite of that, he had to finish his work. He had great confidence, great faith in God. Noah's life was full of persecution and rejection – he was entirely alone. But he couldn't cast off God, though he had to forget all others. His wife and children might have felt sometimes that they would have liked to kill him. But the more he received persecution from his environment, the more whole his heart for God became. He became separated from his circumstances and his community. He became separated from the world, so he came into the position where he could receive God's love. If he had rejected those people who persecuted him, then God's will wouldn't have been fulfilled. But Noah sacrificed himself for those who persecuted him. Instead of causing them to suffer, Noah had a mind to forgive their sins for God. He was standing in the position of the unfallen brother asking God to forgive the fallen brother and sister and willingly bearing all the difficulties. Noah had such a heart. Because of that heart God could proceed in His providence of restoration. The position of complete self-denial centered on God – that was Noah's position.

This same principle can be applied elsewhere – for example, in the cases of Moses and John the Baptist. Moses went the same course. He spent his youth in the Pharaoh's palace. But when he saw his people suffering, he left the Pharaoh's palace. He killed an Egyptian who persecuted Israelites. Moses' position was to save Israel, in spite of the danger. But the people of Israel didn't receive Moses, who tried to save them. They persecuted him, and expelled him to the wilderness of Midian. There for 40 years Moses longed for God, loved God, and made a resolution to save his people. Because of that intention, God chose him to free the Israel people from Egypt.

Let's look at John's life. At the time of his ministry as recorded in the Gospels, he was 30 years old, a young man eating nuts and honey in the wilderness – just like a hippie. He came out of his home and left his relatives behind, thinking of the will of God. In the Bible we read that John ate locusts and wild honey. But his life must have been painful in the wilderness. Do you think he lived solely on locusts and wild honey? It can't be. If you have been to Israel, you know that it isn't a land which would yield much honey. Therefore, he acted like a beggar, going from home to home. Many children followed him, jeering at him. But his mind was concentrating on the idea of the Messiah's coming, and he looked for God's love in the form of the Messiah. So his life was worthy of God's sympathy, and he could stand in the position of witnessing to the Messiah. Though he had been led by God to do this, he was in a position to complain about his situation if he had wanted to. We know he did not care about the problem of detour around material things, but instead he thought, "How can I open a new door?" That's the point where he was great.

Perhaps some of you are thinking, "Why struggle to believe in God? If He exists, He will come down and make a connection with me." If God could do this, we would already be one with Him. That would be fine. But as fallen people, we have no automatic relationship with God. Still, God is the Subject; we are created to be His good objects, though we are not yet in that association. Subject and object should have some kind of close inter-action. We don't have it between ourselves and God. Under these circum-stances you cannot say, "Why believe in God?" We have at least a minimum standard of relationship we must endeavor to reach on our part. Let us take an analogy: In some university a certain professor may be knowledgeable in a certain subject area. But in order to have the opportunity to learn from him, you need to conform to an objective standard; you first must register for his course. Otherwise, the professor and the student have no connection. Naturally certain subjects and objects fit together. They have similar angles, a meeting point, complementary natures, and so on. Otherwise it would not be possible for the professor and the student to relate to each other at all. Nevertheless, their relationship is not automatic.

Between the Subject and yourselves – fallen people, the object – if God decides something, because He is an absolute God, what He decides is eternal and unchanging. He sets the standard. Can you meet His standard if you change your mind a hundred times a day? And another example: You come here and become very inspired when you hear our lectures, but when you go back into the reality of the world, you will have doubts. How long will this inspiration last? God is eternal. He never alters His course in the middle. Even if you make a determined effort, how long will you continue? A month, a year, several years, ten years? Your determination also will change. Some-times you say to yourself, "If I like it, then I will go and do it. If not, then I will not do it." Truth is truth whether you live or die; it is eternal. Truth is beyond death, beyond changeability. In order to be a true person you have to be beyond death. You must have the quality of steadfastness. This means there will be a collision at some point between your changeability and un-changeability. Unchanging elements will overcome changing elements. Changing elements will vanish. Life and death will collide. When you over-come death you will have life. If you pass through this stage then you will have a connection with God. Then when will the moment of truth come for you? It will be the time when there appears an opportunity to be unchanging and changing at the same time. A life and death situation will appear. This is a time of confrontation and challenge. That is when the truth emerges.

Unfortunately, when we live in this world, we like to remain as we are. Also, we don't want to die, or we don't want to be defeated in the reality of this world. The secret to overcome this situation, to find the eternal truth, is to overcome death and come to life, to overcome changeability and become unchangeable. Only in this way can you reach the truth. But this world it-

self wants to remain like it is and does not want to die. This is simply because evil forces dominate this world.

Then, in this connection, what are the Last Days? They are days of rad-
ical transformation taking place in this world of reality. In these days the
world will be running to destruction; people will find no hope, only despair.
Out of this chaos and trouble must come God's children, an element unchanging and beyond death. This eternal element will exist amid the chaos.
A collision will take place, when we come to this situation, and one of the
two elements will be eliminated from the world. Changeability must go and
the eternal quality will remain. When a completely faithful person appears in
this world, since God is Himself unchanging, then He will come down to dwell
with him among the people on earth and help them. He will remain eternally
with us when He sees the chaotic world begin to center itself on the Source of
life, the Source of eternity.

So because God's essence is this absolute standard, to be His object we
have to copy that pattern, meet that standard. We have to ask ourselves if we
qualify to meet His criteria. In order to find whether or not you are qualified, you must be tested through suffering and hardship. You may sometimes
think a certain test is too hard for you, but when you look at it in a different
way, this is the means through which God will give you the chance to prove
your value. And when you pass the test with a perfect score, that means the
Teacher has given you one chance to promote yourself. Usually a teacher
asks those questions which he thinks the students do not know. Why ask
them what they already know? Usually test questions any professor gives are
designed to bring the most qualified person out. To do that he picks the
toughest questions. When you have passed the test and are at the top, then
you and the professor immediately have a certain relationship. The professor values you especially because you have made it through the test, and he
can bequeath all his legacy of knowledge and work to you. If after many
years, he finds only one person who can pass the test, then naturally that person would become the heir of this professor.

God is doing the same thing with us. He would not want us just to be
businessmen or salesmen. He is not interested in that. He wants to find His
loving children, to make you His true sons and daughters. When this relationship is really established, it is inviolable. Nothing can invade that. God
feels so sorrowful that this oneness of love was lost by the fall. He has been
working through the Restoration Providence to find people on earth who
understand this.

So this God will lead you on earth who know Him to the ultimate
point, where He can do something for you. He called Noah long ago, but in
the middle of his course, Noah failed. Abraham, Moses and John the Baptist

all failed to fulfill God's entire hope for them. So He wants people on earth today, including yourselves, to be superior to those men of the past. God's desire is for you children to quickly pass the test. Therefore, He must let you have intense suffering in a short period of time. It took Abraham many years just to establish faith in God. God must ask you quickly to pass the test of suffering and hardship to the same degree. He wants to have your time shortened. For the unchanging God to find the unchanging children, He must test you in a changing situation. God sometimes appears Himself as a capricious God, but this is from your point of view only. Sometimes you are led in contradictory ways to what you had been taught before. It may look like God is changing, but He has a purpose behind this. In order to find unchanging children He must test you in a changing situation.

So when the eternally living God comes to you, He will look like He is leading you into death. It is a test. So the God of life seems like a God of death, in order to restore His children. In the early ages of Christian history, we see this method: God appears to inspire only martyrdom. Through this paradoxical way, He has been restoring people. So we can easily imagine that all the 2000 years of Christianity will be tested; all mankind will be tested in the Last Days.

At that time only one man, only one direction, only one faith will come out to restore all things. God begins His work of creation or recreation always at one central point and expands from there. Centered around the Lord of the Second Advent, the number of God's children will gradually multiply to save the whole world. When Satan discovers the person on the earth who is centered on God, he is afraid of him. There is no way for Satan to accuse or defeat this kind of person.

Christianity appears to be fading in the world today. The world itself seems to be sinking. Even the United States, this gigantic nation, has lost its direction. What is God looking for in this age? He cannot work through the people who accept the world and adapt to it as it is. He looks for the people who never deviate from His standard in this deviated world. He is looking for the people whose faith is so strong that they believe, "Even if the world perishes, we will not." That is the kind of person God is looking for. They will create a new world. This is what God expects from His sons and daughters on earth.

If someone says, "Even without God's help we are going to complete our mission," then what will happen? When people with that attitude appear, then of course God must call these people to His side. There are two kinds of people in this respect – those who do the right things without God's direction, and those who always need God to say, "Do this, do that." Bold people will automatically come out to awaken existing churches of this world to the new reality.

If there is a philosophy through which we can embrace all things of faith and reality, naturally this philosophy will cover the earth. Then the time will come.

Very soon this kind of ideology centering on God will suddenly spring up to embrace the whole universe, enveloping all other systems of thought. Now the life of faith looks intangible and unreal, but it is in fact the eternal and substantial one. While the reality of this world is vivid and can be sensed, it cannot be trusted; it is ephemeral and inconstant. The life of faith in God has the quality of constancy. So this means the life of faith and the reality of the world are opposite. There are several aspects in which this is concretely true. For one thing, in the life of faith you have to be recognized first by God. Secondly, you must always surpass the spiritual standards of past saints and sages. Thirdly, even though saints in the historical dispensation courses may have failed in their missions, you must succeed in your course. Finally, in the past, God gave man help and direction; in this age He expects us to do things by ourselves.

Good sons and daughters will recover everything and return it to God without asking His help. Then you yourself will have liberated God. Restoration will be complete when these sons and daughters restore their heavenly Father's sorrow and bring Him joy. Then He will feel that genuine, pure love is possible again, like that which existed before the fall of man. He will be happy to receive His true sons and daughters. God will automatically welcome you to come to His bosom.

When you have trouble, don't ask Him to help you. Instead you should say, "Father, help the whole world." This kind of attitude of heart is similar to that where there are many brothers, and one brother says to their parents, "Instead of helping me, please take care of my brothers and sisters." That kind of attitude is so precious to the parents. It is quite proper in the ordinary family that such a son might get up early and talk to his parents while the other children are still in bed. That's also the way God's children make a good relationship with Him. The parents will take this child into their confidence. The same thing applies to God and His children. This son naturally will become the center, the heir, the object to his parents. They can speak with him even about secret things. This is the standard of intimacy we are striving for with God. When you do face suffering you yourself have to overcome it. You have to look at the overall situation and determine how to deal with it.

When you walk along the street, why don't you take God's point of view? You have to notice the evil things you would want to change, and then the good things you will multiply for your nation and for mankind. When you look at things this way, through God's eyes, you will be always growing. When you look at the weakness of the political situation, when you look at the changing elements from God's position, you should think, "I am going to reform this and that." If nobody else does it, think in your own mind, "I will do it." When you maintain this kind of disposition, automatically angels and saints will come to you and help you even if you never ask for help from God. Wherever you go, you do not have to worry. You are perfectly all right even in the most dangerous of situations. With this confidence you can overcome any difficulties. Then God will reveal to you in many ways what is going to take place in the world, through dreams or visions or inspiration. This will be very comforting to you in this world of change.

We are all at the end of the world. Because we know this, we should be different from the rest of mankind. We are at the frontier of the world of reality, so we must be prepared to suffer the most.

In the past life in faith, a person came to believe in something. At this time your life in faith will come to have actual reality. Far beyond the world and far beyond the standard of past faith, anything is possible at this stage. Historical men of faith worked hard, but all the accumulated good did not belong to them; they gave everything to us. When we believe and bring their hope into reality by our work, their merit becomes ours. Now your spiritual accomplishments are your own. Therefore, a life of faith can be a life of reality. Very soon, the age of the four-dimensional world will appear. Many spiritual phenomena will take place on earth, and the whole world will be influenced by spiritual experience. The realm of faith and the world of reality will unite.

Up to now Satan and his following have been the dominating forces on earth. Now we must establish the sovereignty of good. New generations, a new age, a new civilization will be created, and very soon we will have the kingdom of God on earth. In the past, ideological systems ended up with only ideals. But now our belief system will bear fruit in actual reality. We have to have pride in that, because we have something tangible in our faith – a reality far above past conceptions and the previous life of faith.

The Basis of Good and Evil

Each of us is either on the side of good or on the side of evil. Any individual, any family, tribe, or nation — as well as the world itself — is on the side of evil or on the side of good. There are many countries in the world, and each nation thinks that it is on the side of goodness. This is because any nation is a group of individuals. Individuals have the tendency to think of themselves as being good, so the nation also has the tendency to think it is on the side of good. But what is the basis to define good and evil absolutely? We all know that all nations or individuals cannot be on the side of good. There must be a way to discriminate between what is good and what is evil.

Young people are apt to say, "If we are inclined to evil, it is because the society and the people around us are evil." They want to shift the responsibility to the outer world. Whatever we say about the world, or nation, they are the aggregate form of individuals, and in the end everything about them depends on the condition of the individual. It is always a question of whether the individual is on the side of good or evil because society consists of individuals. However good the whole world may be, if you as an individual are evil, then society has a great problem. However evil the surrounding circumstances may be, if you are on the side of good absolutely, you will not be influenced. The conclusion is that only if individuals are on the side of good can the society become good.

Any individual has his own view of value, his own view of life — his own view of everything. Anyone who thinks that he is influenced by his society complains about what the society is. It is the intrinsic nature of human beings to be receptive to things they take delight in and to be repulsed by things they do not like. If you are on the side of good and insist on being good, that is all right. But if you are on the side of evil and insist that you are good, that is bad. Since families, societies, communities, nations and the world consist of individuals, one can discriminate among their characteristics just as one can find differences among individuals. There are endless varieties.

Also, as an individual, you are changing every moment. You are not what you were in the morning this afternoon or evening. Likewise, you are different from what you were in your childhood, and you are going to be still different from what you are now. If so, we cannot definitely call ourselves good or evil at any one point, because we continue to change. If we find ourselves ever varying according to the environment and circumstances, then we must doubt our own selves. We have to be skeptical about the individual's basis to define good and evil.

If we as human beings are to define what is good and evil, also since we tend to be self-centered we cannot rely on our own definition.

You have probably never experienced being imprisoned. In prison, every criminal thinks that the society is bad and that he has not done anything to be condemned for. He concludes that he has done such and such a thing in order to make society better – or at least for some honorable purpose. This can happen because we accept no common standard of whether a thing is good or bad. Nevertheless, any human definition cannot hold for long; it cannot be an eternal one. Even though you may think that something you have done is wrong, when other people point out the wrong you have done, you don't like it. You are pleased, on the other hand, when people say you have done a good thing even though you inwardly think that you have done wrong. We cannot give the ultimate definition of good and evil ourselves because of our self-centeredness.

People in general base their definitions of good and evil on human conscience. But, although every person has a conscience, the standard varies from one person to another. If there are one thousand people, there are one thousand varieties of conscience. According to your standard of conscience, you can feel something is good or bad. But can human conscience be the absolute standard of defining good and evil?

Also, you can see law functioning in any nation. By obedience or disobedience to the law, one is thought to be either good or evil. In America there is a constitution. In any unit of community there is some kind of law, including the unwritten law in one's family. But the purpose of setting up laws in Communist nations, for example, and the purpose of setting up laws in the democracies are entirely different from one another. In carrying out national purpose according to Communist ideology, they wouldn't mind using any means at all. But in the democratic world we cannot exercise cruel laws to govern people at their own accord. Since those two powers aim for purposes in opposite directions, we cannot expect either of them to be the final ideology which can include the other. We can finally say that we cannot rely on either of them to provide the final goal which all human beings are headed for.

There are progressive changes taking place in the world. So we can imagine something of higher dimension [than either democracy or Communism] must emerge to express universal purpose. Anything vacillating, fluctuating, or changing cannot be thought of as our ultimate goal. The ultimate standard of good must be set up as the goal for all human beings to attain. However, since we are living apart from such ultimate good, it is difficult to adjust ourselves toward the real and ultimate goal. Any individual must first be able to have a solid foundation of goodness in order for him to go straight forward to the goal of goodness. Therefore, in order for the individual to progress, the ground of goodness must be set up on the individual level. This is not an easy task.

In this world, any individual, any family, any nation may be in the position of an enemy to the others. We are at constant odds with each other, inwardly and outwardly. So we cannot take any basis previously set up as the ultimate basis for the definition of goodness. It cannot be defined in that way. Suppose there exists what seems to be a definition of goodness. People who are on one side may take delight in that explanation, but the people on the other side may oppose it. We are in need of a standard which both sides can recognize. The basic criteria for the definition of good must not be the kind that can be opposed by anyone. It must be of the nature which neither of two parties can deny, but which both can recognize and agree with. Then we can safely come to the conclusion that any definition of goodness must be able to gain equal or overall recognition by all the people of the world. What is the nature of such a definition, then? Any definition which has been made out of self-centeredness and out of self-interest or that is based on a partisan view can never be accepted as the final one.

THE DEFINITION OF GOODNESS

Then we can say that it is goodness to pour out your efforts to win something or to do something for the sake of the public, for the sake of something bigger or better than the individual. That is a safe definition. If that is true, then everyone in the world will come to have the same opinion. Even if Japan and America, for example, were in the position of enemies to each other, they could not oppose this definition. In that case, the Japanese people could say that it is for the sake of the United States that they were acting. And the United States could say that they were doing such and such a thing for the sake of Japan. From human ethics we can say that when you do good things for the sake of other people, that is goodness. Finally, we can say that goodness is acting for the benefit of other people and not for oneself.

From this definition we can determine whether we as individuals, families, groups and nations, are either good or evil. We can say that something being done for the sake of other people is always good. If anyone denies that, then there can be no such word as "goodness." When you say that someone is good, then without exception, that person is doing something that benefits other people. On the other hand, if that person is doing something for his own good at the expense of other people, you can immediately say that that person is evil. The motive of any good individual, good family, or good unit of society is to do things for the sake of others.

Then what is the basis for defining good and evil? Where does it lie? It does not exist in the outside world, but within the individual, in yourself. In case someone is doing something for you, that person stands in the position of good, not you. In order for you to be good, you must be the motivation or origin of carrying out good things. No matter how good your environment may be, this does not mean that you yourself are necessarily good.

The basis of the definition of good and evil lies in yourself. Everything starts from you as an individual. If you are doing things for the sake of others, you may be called good. I have used many words, but the definition is very simple, and the people of the world have still not quite realized that. You may freely say things and do things, but if you do those things for yourself, you are not good. However beautiful a song you may sing for someone, if you are doing that out of greed for their praise or out of jealousy of others, you are not good. If you do things out of arrogance, out of pride in yourself, you are not quite doing things right. Arrogance has nothing to do with goodness.

Even when you sleep, if you do that for your own sake and you think, "I have worked more than other people and I deserve to rest," then in that case, you are not good. Everybody may think that freedom is more than life, but if you enjoy freedom out of greed and for your own sake, you are doing wrong. So it is important that we be able to understand what is good and what is evil.

Let us give an example in the case of Japan [speaking to the Japanese members present]. If Japan goes on being economically abundant, if the Japanese go on developing their economic life for the sake of your own Japan, you deserve the title of "economic animal." At the end you are going to be the enemy of the other people of the world. If the Japanese people made their wealth for the sake of the whole world, even though all the people of Japan would have to perish in doing so, their spirit would endure and last long. They would never perish if they were living that way. Even if they fell into poverty again by going this way, people from other nations would help them because they had been working for the sake of other nations.

In this world when you want to marry, you look for someone who is going to be good to you. That person is in the position of good because he is going to do something for you. No one wants a self-centered person. You know very well that if you do things for the sake of your spouse, you are a good person. And if he or she serves you and does things for you, you are ready to do good things in return. If you want to serve other people, and if both of you have that attitude, then your family will be receiving. Therefore, when you want to serve your spouse and do things for the sake of your counterpart, you will gain something in return. However, if you are both greedy, then neither will receive the affection of the other. Everything will break apart. So we reach the conclusion that good will prosper and increase while evil will diminish and die.

Then are you ready to be good or bad? Every person in the world would want to be good. There is not a single person who would dream of being ruined. If we really knew that when we do things for others we will ourselves prosper, there would be no one who would not follow the way of goodness. Good will last forever.

The standard of good must be something really eternal and unique. I want you to have a clear understanding of what is good. You must be seeing things for the sake of others, not for your own sake. You must lend your attentive ears and listen to everything for the sake of other people, not for the sake of yourself. You should be talking, acting out things and using all your five senses for the sake of others and not for yourself. If you found anyone living like that, you would long to be with that person, even to see him – all of him, his eyes, his nose, his mouth, his whole being. You would feel great affection towards that person. The fruit of good deeds will be affection from others and good accomplishments. If you find a person doing things for his own sake, saying things and thinking things all for his own benefit, there will be no such thing as love functioning or arising around him. If you at all love that kind of person, eventually you will regret it.

The definition of goodness we have given must be in accordance with history and present world situations, as well as with the life of future generations. It will continue to be true. I must repeatedly say that your eyes are not created for yourself. Eyes are for the sake of seeing something objective. You talk because you have someone to talk to. You cannot say you are happy without anyone around you. When I speak, if you in the object position are happy to hear me, I become more and more elevated in spirit. When I am eagerly talking to you and you don't listen to me attentively, I lose my spirit and don't want to talk any longer. Even when you touch something, would you take more delight in touching your own hand or touching the hand of your lover? You would rather want to touch the skin of your lover than your own. So it is wrong to think that you have your five senses for your own sake. They exist for the sake of others.

Why is it that anything good must take place for the sake of other people? You probably think at first, "I don't like the idea of having to work for the sake of other people in order to be called good. If I could do things for myself and be thought good, how wonderful it would be." We are born that way, so it cannot be helped.

We are created for the sake of other people. For instance, any masculine being is not created for himself, but for the sake of the opposite sex. Man was created for the sake of woman. Suppose there is a beaufitul girl. Would she want to live forever with another beautiful girl? No, she would look for a handsome man, and she would think that her beauty is for the sake of that man. If there are two beautiful girls living together, rather than being attracted to each other, they would repulse each other. Suppose there is just one man for the two beautiful girls, and that man is an unattractive person. Both women would want that man for her husband, nevertheless. Our conclusion is that men and women are born for the sake of each other.

The very motivation of God in creating man is for the sake of woman, and woman for the sake of man. That being the truth, we can safely say that when we do things for other people, that is absolutely defined as good. When we call a family a happy one, that home is the place where the couple is living in good harmony with each other, not fighting. When they give birth to their children, their children would think that their parents are the best ones in the whole world. If a couple would live in perfect harmony with each other, their family would be thought of as the best family in the whole neighborhood, the whole community, and the whole nation.

THE ORIGIN OF GOODNESS

God made man out of His love, out of goodness. Goodness is something which was there before our birth. So after our birth too, the motivation of our doing things for others is repeatedly always to do good. Then why is good defined as things to be done for the sake of other people? Who made things that way?

When man was created, did he spring into being as he is all by himself, with that law of goodness within him? The motivation did not come from himself. Some Reality, some Being of higher dimension defined him. That Something, that Reality said, "Let there be a man, let there be a woman," and that Being made those two for the sake of goodness. No result can come about without cause. When we think that ultimate Being set up the basis of goodness in the beginning, then we can safely say that the first Cause or Reality was good. Whatever we may call Him, that Being must be the ultimate Good. Man began to call him "God." What is God? What is He like?

Since God created man for the sake of other people, then God must be doing things for the sake of man. Because He is the Cause and we are the result of His creation, then the Cause must be something like the result. If God exists, He must be living for the sake of something or someone other than Himself. In human society, too, the more you do things for the sake of others, the more good you become. If you keep doing that, doing things for other people, you will come closer and closer to the central point – God. In a community, if you do things for the sake of the public, in the long run you will become the leader in that community. Even though you may be reluctant, unwilling to be there, some force will drive you to the central point. When you elect your president, senators and congressmen, you want to choose someone who will do something for the people of the nation. If he is the type of person who is not acting to serve others, he would be a dictator, and you wouldn't want him to have such a position.

If there is a person who is going to do things for the sake of other people through eternity, never changing, then he is going to be the central personage to lead the people with him through eternity. If there is any Being, any Reality, who is going to do things for the sake of the universe, he is going to be the central point through eternity, and this is God. We can call this kind of God the true God and the Standard of real and everlasting goodness. God created man in His likeness and image, so we, originally, are supposed to serve others. If we go on doing this through eternity, we can say that we are temples of God, resembling Him.

God, in creating the universe, did that for man. Likewise, when we create anything, we must be doing it for others. However beautiful a voice you may have, if you sing all by yourself with no one around to hear you, you are not really happy. The same is true when you dance. You want to dance for the sake of other people, for them to see you and join you when you dance. So the word "happiness" itself can assume any meaning when there is someone else to appreciate it.

Peace is also that way. Peace, equality, anything of virtue cannot come about all by itself. Freedom too is not something you can enjoy by yourself. When you are all alone, there is nothing which you can call valuable or happy. There must be purpose to be free, to be equal, to be ideally happy. So you must have an object to be really happy. If you have your object and there is reciprocal action, then there is circular movement. If the action of give and take is there making circular motion, if it circles intensely enough, it will result in three-dimensional action. There is no real front or back, right or left; it is like the axial rotation of a plane when it revolves around so fast as to make entire oneness.

Unification also cannot come about all by itself. There must be something in the object position to be unified. If those in the object and subject positions work alone, the action cannot come about. Now we clearly know that God created man to think, to speak and to act for the sake of other people. We know that everything belongs to God. God wants someone to whom He can give out all He has. Anything in God's possession is for the whole world. If God found someone who was ready to do things for the sake of the whole world, God would be ready to give out all He had to that person. In giving things to that person, God is most willing. He is not reluctant.

The very beginning of man's relationship to God was like this. God was willing to give all He had to man, and man was willing to return all he had to God. If that kind of relationship were permanently established by all individuals in the world, the whole world would be in beautiful harmony. God, as the core of such harmony, would take delight in living in human society.

However unassuming a man may be, he would want to be the center of the whole world if he had such a possibility. When man finds God or ultimate Being, he wants to possess that Reality or that Being all for himself. We are so greedy as not to want to share that Being with each other. But we are in the position of minus. That is, we are something like a vessel to contain what is coming from God. So, if you are a big vessel, a round and perfect one, God will fill your cup. There must be perfect individuals, perfect families, perfect nations and a perfect world. On the broader level, the perfect man becomes the central personage. God would want to give all He had to that person. God has to find that kind of person. If such a person cannot be found, God will recreate him and send him to the world, because He is seeking to give out all He has to humanity through that channel.

Out of the greed of man and the Archangel, the human fall came about. Not only the Archangel, but Eve and Adam wanted to have things for themselves. This caused the fall. The intrinsic nature of God was unselfishness about doing things for the sake of others. But instead of multiplying God's nature, human beings after the fall began to do things in the opposite manner – for their own sakes. We are the very descendants of the fallen ancestors. So we are the other way around from what God intended us to be.

Though our intrinsic nature is something good, we are more inclined to do evil things. There is a voice from our conscience telling us to do things for the good of others. But in some people, even the conscience is accelerating their doing things for themselves. In general, our consciences are closer to God than our fleshly demands or desires. If you know that there is a boundary between good and evil, then do you find yourself having gone beyond the boundary to join the side of good? You, yourself, know the answer very well. You don't have to apply constitutional law or any other kind of law to decide that. You can immediately and accurately determine whether you are on the side of good or of bad. Inwardly, you know how to distinguish good from evil. So you must remove the evil and cultivate the good within yourself. Selfishness, self-centeredness – those are your greatest enemies. You must be able to resist those powers and you must be ready to do things for the sake of other people. Make your all-out effort to do good things and you will come to resemble God. Then you will take delight in what you are doing, and God will be pleased with you.

THE ROLE OF RELIGION

God established many religions in the world because He wanted to drive the people to the side of good through religious teachings. If you recognize the fact that there are many such religions leading people to the side of goodness, you cannot deny that God is working behind the scenes of history. There is no doubt of that. God exists. Since God is absolute and omniscient and omnipotent, it must be possible to restore the original position.

There was a purpose for God's creating man. Then in order for us to fulfill that original purpose, God will help us. Without our being able to do that, God's entire purpose of creation will be nullified. Without working through man, God cannot establish His kingdom on earth. God Himself created the world and whatever things are good for the sake of man. So man must be able to establish His kingdom on earth. Then God's hope is to find a man with the personality of ultimate good, who can establish for Him the kingdom of God on earth.

If there is any ideology, any doctrine, any "ism" or any religion that is going to accomplish that mission to establish God's kingdom on earth, God will rely upon the group surrounding such a way of thinking. God is in the position of the ultimate or cosmic Subject, so He would want a person of that value, of His dimension, to work through; a person of that quality would be what God would have to have. From God's side there are no national boundaries. There is no discrimination among individuals. Any and every individual has equal right to claim God and to have equal value. There must come into being an individual or a group of people with God's way of thinking. They will resemble God and must restore themselves back into the original position. There are many countries in the world, but none of them is completely in accord with God's will. There are many religious groups existing in the world, but none of them is up to His standard. Therefore there must appear a group of people under a religious view or ideology that will be in conformity with God's will. God is most anxious to find such a people, such a nation.

We must recognize that we ourselves are here to carry out the mission for the sake of all mankind, for the sake of God's will. With that confidence fused in our minds we must be brave and bold enough to go through any difficulty. If we go on like this, all the heavenly destiny will be on our side and will push us ahead. Sooner or later we will attain our goal, and then we will be one with God Himself. If we are in the object position to the ultimate Subject, God, then we are placed in the central point of the universe. And all the universe is destined to come close to us and be united with us.

If you are in that position, you are the center of yourself as an individual, of your family, of your tribe, of your nation, and of the world. God's essence, or the core of goodness inherent in God, will come through you as an axis to turn the whole world. Since you are doing all things for the sake of other people, you are in the central point, and since you are in the central point, you are the basis of goodness. God will work through you to move the world. You will have nothing to do with the basis of evil. In that case you are doing things in accordance with the purpose of the principle of creation. You are the instrument carrying out God's will, and you are doing things which God would want you to do. In that case, you are enjoying the value of the man that God originally created. By taking that responsibility on yourself, you become indispensable to God, and you are naturally placed in the central position. You are going to be the basis of good; you have nothing to do with evil. That kind of person is what God would want to have.

So if you are resolved to eat and sleep and do all things for the sake of mankind, then you can never be invaded by evil power. For some it may take a lifetime to become a man of such personality, but if we know the Principle, we will want to be that kind of person. We want to build that kind of personality in ourselves within seven years, or if possible, in one year or less. Even though we have to pay a tremendous toll of indemnity, we want to go that way. If you want to be that kind of person, you will have to suffer a great deal. We must be ready to go through as much as necessary.

There is selfishness and individual-centeredness in the United States and the world today. In the midst of all problems we must become the core of this society, cleaning up everything ugly. There is a great challenge ahead of us. We are going to attack everything evil and drive it out of this country and the world. From the definition we have just given, we are sure that we can win over the evil forces in this country. If we work strenuously, we will succeed. We want to carry out the tradition of our heavenly Father. God has been working all through the 6000 biblical years of providential history, day and night without rest, for the sake of all mankind. If we have inherited His will, can we not do that? Has God been complaining that He has had to work so hard? He knows that however great the difficulty He has had to go through, it is nothing compared with what will have been achieved at last. So we have to resemble Him and struggle hard to attain the goal.

Since God is omnipotent and we resemble God, if we leave anything undone, it is because we have not struggled enough. If we have struggled in wholehearted effort to attain the goal, nothing like despair, distress or complaint are possible. Instead of those, we will pour out all our energy, all our beings into this cause, and we will be successful. There is nothing like evil existing on God's side. There is only progress possible, only victory possible on God's side. If you really know that you have inherited that kind of tradition from God as the children of God, then you can't complain to Him about what you have to do. That's impossible. We must be indignant about the existence of evil and want to eradicate its last remnants. On the solid foundation of good which God has set for us, we want to eliminate all evil from the individual, from the family, from the whole society. After removing evil elements from ourselves, we must purify the whole world.

You must be resolved to be one who is to shoulder the responsibility to purify the world, promoting goodness, having nothing to do with evil. I want you to be like that, and I am confident that you are going to fulfill your mission.

In such an awareness that you are on the side of good, inheriting God's tradition, I want you to do things for the great cause of God, purifying all mankind. This being the leading nation of the world, you are going to work here. I want you to be victors for this cause.

May God Protect Us

No matter who you are, you are not born from an act of your own will. From birth to a certain age you don't realize your purpose of life or your role in life. It is not until you reach your adolescence that you begin to consider your purpose in life, think about what kind of life you are going to lead, and learn about the nature of human society as a whole. After going through the stage of adolescence, you enter the prime stage of youth, where your philosophy of life will become fully developed. However, only in old age will your view of life become fully ripened, and your understanding of what life really is become clear.

Any one individual cannot live all alone, centered on himself. In order for us to live, we need our friends, our family and our neighbors and society around us. Broadening our scope, we can live life on the national level, and finally on the world-wide level. Each man struggles hard to become an important person, and at best a figure of historical importance. Only a few can attain this high goal, while most others cannot reach this level. Most people pass into the spirit world after their physical death without being able to attain this goal. This is the common way of life for all men, and the destiny of humanity.

However, we see many different types of people who walk on the path of life. Some go straight forward, some go sideways, some go backwards, while some others go in a zig-zag line. The record you make by your life is like lines which are traced behind you. Though you are still young, when you look back to your past, there must have been happy days and unhappy days, easy days and difficult days, meaningful days and days full of regret. From the viewpoint of your own interest, I'm sure that you have experienced more unhappy days than happy ones because of the unfavorable environment which exists in the world today. Very likely you are not in the position to be proud of yourself even though you may have confidence in what you do. Nobody can tell what will happen in the next moment. That has been the nature of our destiny as human beings.

In other words, you may go to work in the morning with happy anticipation, but nobody can guarantee your safety throughout the day. Even though your office may be nearby, you can never be too confident, because even a short distance from your doorstep you may have a car accident. Nobody can tell what our destiny holds for us. You can even meet seemingly agreeable people in seemingly agreeable places, but the result is not necessarily good – it could even bring untold misery to you. Passing an examination may be the goal of people who study hard. But at the very moment that a person finds he has passed the exam, some tragedy could happen. Nobody can tell. Suppose there are a man and a woman who dearly love each other, and they are confident that they are going to live as the most ideal couple in the whole world. But right at the wedding ceremony, something unexpected may come about. From this we can gather that a man can never be too sure of having a bright future. There are many instances in the world in which we are compelled to go the way opposite to what we would have if we were left to our own choice. We may think that life belongs to us, but we find that we are not always free to run our lives as we wish. That's how it is with human life. Thus, we are walking on the path of life without confidence, not knowing what we may find on the way. We are groping in darkness every day of our lives, in search of a flickering hope which promises to provide something good.

But there are not too many things around us that hold such a promise for goodness. Things are usually the other way around; we find more tragedy than goodness. Then, is there a place where we can be relaxed and reassured? No one can be relaxed and reassured when he is all alone. You need someone who can at least defend and protect you. Who must that someone be? Your parents may be able to play this role externally, protecting you to a certain extent. But they cannot guarantee your life in the face of death. Your teachers cannot take this responsibility; neither can your friends nor your nation, with all its power. Suppose the whole world is mobilized to help you; it cannot take responsibility for your life. Then, who can take the responsibility? We must find someone who can do that. Otherwise we are sure to be insecure and unhappy, even though we want to be happy and at ease.

We want someone to protect us on our way of destiny. Then, what must that someone be like? This one must transcend history; that is, the past, present and the future. He must transcend time and space. Unfortunately, man himself cannot transcend these no matter how great he is. Therefore, we are badly in need of someone like that who can take responsibility for our life in faith. If we cannot find one like that in human society, we would want to create someone in our imagination and fancy that he would protect us. But if there really is such an entity, how happy we would be! How eager we would be to locate him. The more difficult the environment becomes, the more insecure we become and we ardently set off in search of him. In this situation, unless you endeavor to confirm his existence and enter into a good relationship with him, you can never be assured about your life.

Then, what kind of relationship would you want to have between God and yourself? There may be teachers who are our seniors and who can pro-tect us with their position, wealth and knowledge. But it is more desirable that we have someone who would protect us with the warmth of love. If we are going to be protected at all, we want to be protected not just for the time being, but for eternity. Then, who in the world could do that? Our parents. We need our parents. Next, we need brothers and sisters, and we also need our spouse, then our children. With them, we enjoy the blessedness of our life. But no matter how bright a day may be with other people rejoicing in the blessedness of our surroundings, if someone we love is on the verge of death, we cannot enjoy all the rest. However happy we may otherwise be, if our loved one is in a tragic situation, we, too, become unhappy.

When we look at things from this viewpoint, we can enjoy utmost happiness when we are with our loved ones sharing with each other an ideal love to the utmost degree. We don't know where we are bound in our life, just walking on the way not knowing our destination. We are always in-secure. Centered on our physical parents, happiness will be mortal. The same thing is true centered on our brothers and sisters, and centered on married couples. Love with these people may change and even become ephemeral. Then we must look for and find that ideal love which will last for eternity. There seems to be no such love in the world, but we will never stop looking for it. We especially look for the one who will enable the love between parents and children and love between husband and wife to last for eternity, under his protection. That someone must be unchangeable, unique and eternal — that is, God.

Without God as the center point or starting point, we cannot make all these relationships unchangeable and eternal ones. There must be a person with a central mission as the agent of God's love, around whom all these re-lationships will be restored to their desired form. He must become the mediator between God and man to make that relationship a oneness between Father and son. The relationship must be restored between the parents and the children, between brothers and sisters, between husband and wife, to the original form which God intended at the time of creation. We are in pursuit of this relationship and to fulfill this relationship is the ultimate destiny of our lives. An ideal relationship of true love cannot be an ephemeral one, but is unchanging, unique and eternal.

As I said before, any relationship of love must exist by the relationship between subject and object -- you cannot enjoy love all by yourself. That is to say, everyone needs someone to love and protect him in an ideal environment provided by that person. Then alone can we be really relaxed in an environment which we trust will never change. However hard we may try, we will not find that stability in human society. Everything in human society is temporary and changeable. We need someone absolute and unchanging. He must be an omnipotent one. Therefore, throughout history, man has sought to find God through religious belief. In true religion, we should be able to re-store the true relationship between parents and children, brother and sister, and husband and wife. With this knowledge, would you want to reach God through the mediator, the one who is the perfect object to God, the perfect Subject? Or, would you want to go straight to God? Which would you pre-fer? You are far below the standard at which you should be, and so you must go through the way, and the mediator is this way.

In a sense, a religion is the mediator, because every religion teaches about God. You know that God exists, but in what relationship to God would you want to put yourself? The relationship which is primary and also the most desirable one is the parent-child relationship. So, we want to serve God as our Parent with Him in the subject position, and with ourselves in the object position. Sometimes we want to make God our friend; sometimes we just feel like having Him as our brother. In an absolute love, He can be just anything to us. In that love, a father would not complain if his son would rule over him, although he is still in the position of the father. In the relationship of such love, a husband would never complain against his being dominated by his wife and vice versa. Love alone and nothing else makes it possible. Love is the highest law and the sacred bond bringing any two or more beings into harmonious oneness. However high in authority or in knowledge or wealth we may be, we all become tender and obedient like lambs when we feel such a love. There is no one in the whole world who would refuse this love or look down upon it.

Is there anyone who is not willing to be dominated by that kind of love? Even God is willing to be dominated by that love, not to speak of man.

Love is great. God is the very core of love, which makes Him the greatest of all. Love is the power that motivated God to create man and love alone is what makes God absolute. Centered on love, even the absolute and supreme Being is willing to be at the disposal of one who is the incarnation of His love. To such a man, God is the Father who is willing to become everything else for him. God is the Parent of all parents to man. He has the absolute love that surpasses the love of even model parents. With that love He can embrace all the parents of the world. In fact, God created man from His parental love. Without that love we die.

God is always ready to give the type of love which is best suited to and most wanted by the person seeking a relationship with Him. If we wanted parental love from God, He would be prepared with it; if we wanted brotherly love or conjugal love, or the love of a friend from Him, He is ready with these. He is also the symbol and reality of national love and universal love. In our church, we allow people to understand and feel God's love in such a dimension. Isn't it wonderful that the God of love is protecting us in every possible relationship? We, as the incarnation of His love, can in turn protect others and even ourselves along the way of fate, with this power of God's love.

When we pinch ourselves it hurts. But if we are assured manifold benefits after the pain, will we not gladly endure it? With this confidence, we can dash forward on any path of misery and hardship. Everyone is uneasy and insecure on the way of fate, without knowing what our future has in store for us. If, in this dark situation, we find a light giving us the full and clear picture of where we are bound, how are we going to march forward to the goal where the new world of God-centered love and harmony waits for us? Would we not abandon our old way of life and join the new one? Because of the evil entity, Satan, we have to make the way smooth and straight by repelling the satanic power as we go along and by building the kingdom of God in our hearts and sharing it with our fellow men. God is the ultimate subjective Being, and we as His objects want to work for His sake and ours, and finally find Him and join Him in perfect oneness.

If we are confident of God's love, we can overcome any difficulty, however uneven the road may be. The more difficult the road is, the stronger our conviction is that this is the short-cut through which we reach the goal at the earliest possible date. There we can meet God who is anxiously waiting for us, full of blessings to give those who dash forward with all their knowledge and understanding. Once we do this, misery and unhappiness cannot dominate our lives. Through our everyday experience, we know that without love we cannot overcome the miseries on our way of fate.

Let us suppose that a man died through misfortune on the way of his search for the ultimate subjective Being. However, his death does not mean the end, but the beginning of his life. Then, in the spirit world, this man could tell God even that he died in order to live in the spirit world, to more fully enjoy God's love. We must be ready to die, but to die with God's love in our hearts. If we imagine that we are going to die in the bosom of God's love, then we do not die a miserable death at all. In this case, a man's death could be of higher value than any other death, because he died with the best attitude. If your wife died long ago, and after you had died this kind of invaluable death you joined her in the spirit world, would she not respect and love you more than she had on earth? If you died for the sake of someone, and that person later comes to the spirit world, would he not love and serve you? Their love in the spirit world must be of higher dimension than their love on the earth.

In the Bible we read many paradoxical things. Jesus said, "If you love me, you must deny yourself and bear the cross and follow me." (Luke 17:33) He also said that, "Those who want to gain their lives will lose them." These words encourage us to win the love of highest dimension at the cost of everything else. If you loved me so much as to die for me, and I met you later in the spirit world, how happy we would be to see each other! If you truly love someone, you will always gladly die for him. Even though you might die, it would not mean the end, but it means new life. By this kind of sacrificial death, we pass through the toll gate to reach the world of love, which is eternal and of a higher dimension. Then we are not afraid of love. Are you willing to die that kind of death? When we know what is coming after death, we are happy people, even though we may have to die.

We have all discovered great things. I have gone through untold difficulties, but I am sure I am the happiest man in the whole world – am I not? I am a happy man because I know how to overcome unhappiness with love. I am the type of person who hates to be sympathized with, but I love to sympathize with others, and I feel immense happiness in making others happy. When I want to sympathize with others out of my own accord, can I complain about what I have to do? In this way, I can enjoy the real taste of love. When I am sympathized with, I can only taste passive love, which is not what I want.

Some may think that our faith forces us or drives us on the painful way. But I hope most of you can overcome the pain by digesting it with the power of love, because happiness and love are promised at the end of hardships. As our subject indicates, we want someone to protect us on the way of fate. That someone must be God. But even God cannot protect or love us when we don't deserve it – that is, when we don't set up the condition to receive that love. God is not in need of money, position or knowledge. What He needs is love. And we need that love too, because by true love we can enjoy the privilege of controlling Him. If we can do that, we can control our own fate, because we can control God who controls our fate. God would not leave those who truly love Him on the path of unhappiness and misery. God will help His people to overcome the miseries caused by Satan.

Those who are ardently in love with God can easily overcome unhappiness, because the way of unhappiness will lead them to happiness. When I was in prison in North Korea, I went through severe torture; the more severe the torture was, the stronger I would become. Every cell of mine was mobilized to fight against the pain. I would fancy that with every blow God's blessing would be multiplied. Because of this, I was not afraid of the torture, and I could easily endure it. If we have this attitude, we can make the crooked way straight and the bumpy road smooth. Even though our path of life may be an uneasy, insecure, ephemeral one, full of misery which is more than death, we know that through God's love for us and our love of God, we can go through the path without difficulty. When we are ready to live and die in the love of God, we deserve God's protection. This is the way every human being has to go. May God protect us on our way of destiny.

Three Stages of Judgment

It is our duty as fallen men to pass through three stages of judgment – judgment of words, judgment of personality, and judgment of love or heart.

JUDGMENT OF WORDS

All through history, mankind has been in search of the truth, true words. The truth is the standard by which all the problems of mankind can be solved. We know man somehow fell in the beginning, and to fall means to fall into the bondage of Satan. So in order for us to return to the original position, we have to overcome the bondage of Satan. For fallen people, there is no other message which is more hopeful and desirable than the message of restoration to the position before the fall. To be restored is, in another sense, to be liberated from Satanic bondage–and this is the gospel of gospels for fallen men.

Then, what is judgment? Judgment is the measurement of all our actions according to the original standard. If our acts cannot come into accord with the original rule or measurement, we must be judged or punished. With any government, there is the ruling party and the opposition party, with a balance of power between them. If one of the laws is set up to be amended, then both parties must agree. In the universe there are God and Satan. Between the two there stand men and women–some are more on God's side, and others are more on the Satanic side. But in judging the people there must be a standard of judgment accepted by both God and Satan. People more on the right side can be claimed by God, and on the other side by Satan. In worldly matters too we have a certain standard or rule. If we compare something to that measurement, and if it is above the standard, then it is called successful, for example; but if it is below the standard, then we call it a failure. If it is a total failure, so that it cannot even be compared by measurement, then there can be no judgment possible. Neither God nor Satan can claim this total failure.

In the course of restoration there must be the standard rule. If you are going to find one in the Bible, which must it be? For instance, with any mountain there are peaks and valleys. Centered on one peak, there are two sides; God is on the right side, while Satan is on the other side. There is a difference between the high peaks and the low peaks. All through history, when we examine the courses our ancestors passed through, the process is something like going up a peak, then down, and then again attaining a certain height. In that way, mankind of the past have been generally climbing up. There are many peaks of various heights. Those who belonged to the Old Testament Age began to climb up, and on the peak they decided whether they were on God's side or the Satanic side. Then they made another hike to reach another peak of greater height. The climber begins right at the foot of the first peak, and he passes on what he has attained to the climbers after him. The Messiah is the person who would be waiting on the highest peak, and those who have attained the peak will be welcomed and praised. But the Messiah himself has to know what way they have had to go through.

Jesus is the fruit of the truth, of God's Logos. He has attained the highest peak in the spiritual sense. Jesus said, "The Old Testament came about for me; everything and every word from God is for me." (Matt. 5:17, John 5:39-40) He said on another occasion, "I am the way, the truth and the life." (John 14:6) The way is the truth and the truth is the way and life, too. The truth is something God exalts, while Satan is jealous of it. The truth belongs to God. God must love the law He has set up and He is going to love it through eternity. Then what must be the mission of the truth? The mission of the truth is to guide the people through their way. The Principle of Restoration is to connect all the ways trodden by the Old Testament Age saints with the New Testament Age saints, through the present. We are going to make the zig-zag road a straight one, so that we can show to the people the standard of how to reach the highest peak. The shortest way is the straight line, and the mainstream and the final way. That's what the word "principle" means. What kind of principle is this? What is the Divine Principle?

The Divine Principle is the measure or the way – the guide – that will take us through the path to reach God, and to the original position before the fall. Without going through this way, fallen men cannot reach the original position. This is the measurement, ruler, and fundamental guide. Mankind have walked a tangled way away from God, and we must return through the same path. But we are going to straighten it out. Suppose you had a rope or string entangled with knots. If you just use your strength and pull hard on the ends, would the knots be undone? No. If you spent hours of your time, would that alone solve the problem? Time and energy poured out in blind, random efforts would not do anything. In praying before God, also, if you just pray blindly to Him to give you something or to help you to do something, He can never help you. There must be a rule or standard to be met.

Suppose again there is a very good man, but he is a blind man. Without his knowing how to use a sword, would God give it to him? There is the danger of his grasping the blade instead of the handle. God would not give it to him. If He did, He would be a blind God. Everything must meet its standard. The Divine Principle is the measurement by which God can liberate fallen men. You will be liberated into true words, the truth. You will be liberated from the darkness into the light, where you can see the relationship between God and yourself in precision.

In America you ride in cars every day. When you are in a hurry, you want to speed up. When you go at full speed, there is danger. If you want to speed without danger, then you have to have had good practice beforehand. In handling the steering wheel, is there flexibility? Can you move it just as you please? Not an inch of freedom is there. The wheels of the car must be round; if they are bent, driving will be dangerous. If the four wheels have a will of their own.and some won't turn as they should, what will happen? The air pumped into all of those four wheels must be the same amount or they will not move together properly. If you want to go at full speed, it means the wheels will have to make many revolutions. I know that you may dislike repeating things, the same old things. But when you want to keep a diamond glittering, you have to polish it. If you want to keep this room clean, won't you clean it once, twice or more each day? The same applies to learning the Principle. You must learn the truth well, in every particular.

Have you ever stopped to think how many times in your life you will be talking with people about the truth? When you eat food, it becomes more delicious as you chew it fully. If you just chew once or twice and swallow it, do you know the real taste of the food? With a thing of value, you must repeatedly practice with it and try to know the taste of it, and it will give you more and more. So repetition does not fatigue you. You must know the truth well. The first standard of judgment is that of words. If you do not pass the standard, you cannot be released from bondage.

JUDGMENT OF PERSONALITY

The second is the judgment of personality. However hard you may struggle to walk fast on a certain road, if you are going the wrong way, you have to come back. Where does Satan lie in ambush? He is always close to the main road, the true way. Because he wants to snap you up and stop you from going along the right road, he comes to attack you without warning. So, you must prevent him from stopping you from going on the way. However well-practiced, however well-equipped you may be, if you are attacked by Satan on the way, that is the end of it. You must have a technique to prevent Satan from stopping you. You must have the personality to win over Satanic temptation. You must be more able, stronger than Satan in every way. You must be alert to see where Satan lies in ambush. Have you ever stopped to think of that? Satan is everywhere – and you are vulnerable to his attack. You must know how to locate him and find him out. When you are strong enough not to be tempted or fall into the hands of Satan, you can win over him; but you must know Satan waits for the time when you are about to fall into the pit, when you are in the most difficult situation. That's the moment Satan comes to press on your throat.

When you fight on the battlefield, the enemy lies in ambush. Most likely, he comes to attack you during the night – when you don't expect him. Spies will come, but if you have wide-open eyes, they will run away. When you are in slumber or relaxation, or when you are in distress or despair, that's the time of Satanic attack. For instance, you are frustrated and say to yourself, "Oh, I have worked one year on the mobile team, can I go on like this?" That's the very moment Satan will attack you. Satan would say, "You are my prey at this very time." All you have accomplished before will be gone. It would not take one of the strong Satans [evil spirits] to attack, but the smallest and weakest one can press on your throat and you will be spiritually killed. Isn't that true? When you are in distress, frustrated, you must remind yourself of the fact that this is the very moment when the weakest of Satans can attack you. When you are not witnessing, not doing church work – when you are thinking only of good food, fine clothing – when you are in that kind of mood, that's the very moment you are liable to Satanic invasion. When you miss your sweetheart, that's the very moment Satan attacks you. Those are the hooks on which Satan can drag you back. When you doze off, that means you are in a lax mood. That's the very moment Satan will come and snatch you away. When you cannot help being tired and frustrated, try to go somewhere away from the observation of others. Meditate, pray there for three days, and after doing that you will look at your brothers and sisters working so hard and think, "What am I?" In distress you will think, "Can I be loved by God? I must work." Your conscience will tell you. You will be aroused to new vitality. You pray in repentance, and feel again like going out to work. That's better.

Many times when I was in prison [in North Korea] I would appear in handcuffs before the judge; and on my way from prison to the court, on the street I would sometimes meet members from my church. I would wave my hands at them in hilarious joy. And when I waved my hands, the handcuffs jangled – the noise of it still resounds in my ears.

I swore then I would never die before realizing my mission. I would demonstrate my determination, and I would never stop before that day came. I would be strong enough to endure all difficulties. And when I was released, I would work again with more zeal. I thought even prison was my training course, and that afterward I would be a stronger worker for God. When you picture the prison life, don't ever imagine the prisons in this country. That prison was far below your level – untold misery – almost like animal life. If I were to describe it, you wouldn't understand. We had a handful of rice, almost rotten, each day. We missed good rice and food, and yet we had to work on, mining and loading heavy bags of chemicals. And after we were exhausted and were to receive our handful of rice, on the way to eat some of us would die. Others were so anxious to get rice that they would even take it out of dead men's mouths to feed themselves. At those times I would say to myself, "Even if hardships are doubled and tripled, I will never fail." Even in the Communist prison, I worked so hard that they had to give me a prize for achievement.

I am sympathetic with you. You are in the prime of your life. You want to dance with your sweethearts; you want to enjoy your life in the worldly sense. There are many good things teeming in this world for you. But you have been awakened to the fact that someone must do this job, not just myself. This heavy world is falling to destruction. Some power must stop it. The whole earth is covered with war and misery, and you are living on that earth. Along with it, you know you are going to come to destruction. The merry-makers – those without the knowledge of what is happening – may look happy. But those who know that the world is collapsing cannot help but want to stop it. Some people are indifferent. But would you just stand by and watch the world end? Wouldn't you want to do something about it, even if you had to die or be killed to do so? There may be many casualties, by tens and hundreds of thousands, but if you are not prepared to die for the cause, you cannot live to save the world.

If you are ready to die ahead of others, all of you; if you have that attitude, you will not die and you can save the world. But if you are like the disciples of Jesus who denied him upon his death, you will fall away and the whole world will be left unsaved. Would you become like Jesus' disciples? Jesus' disciples were in fear of Satan and they were overwhelmed by Satanic power. Satan took them away – all twelve disciples, who in Jesus' lifetime had served him. Then, what happened to Jesus? Satanic hands were on him, but he died a physical death, not a spiritual death. If your spirit is not dead, if you have the same zeal and ardor upon your death, there is a way to be saved and resurrected again.

If you have to die, and if you die a courageous death – without leaving shame to your descendants – then you have the chance to be resurrected and work through your descendants. Jesus was attacked by Satanic hands, but he was not defeated by Satan. God, who is more awesome than Satan, was on his side, fighting for him. You must know that. God is on the side of righteousness. Have you ever stopped to think, "How long can I work? Will there be a time when I will be utterly frustrated? " To be shot to death is a simple thing, but to be tortured spiritually, to have Satan cut off every limb – arms and legs – would you bear that torture?

If you are resolved to live for the cause and die for the cause, you are already being resurrected. You are transcending life and death. In that case you are on God's side and God is on your side, because God is also the being transcendent of life and death. God is our Friend and our Co-worker. Those who have God as their co-worker must be courageous. God is not only your friend, but your Father. You are going to be the incarnation of God. God belongs to the whole universe, to all humanity. He sent many saints and prophets to work for the great cause and they were killed and martyred. That means God's hands and arms and all limbs were cut off. He has been enduring pain all the way. But He is still intact from Satanic invasion; He is sane and whole and all-powerful and almighty. He is living in me and I am the incarnation of Him. Would you not be proud and stand as firmly as He is standing? Then, with that quality, will you say you are tired after a year, after five years, ten years, twenty years? Will you be tired of doing this job? When will you be exhausted? Never? In a word, you must think you are born for this life and this is your destiny.

You cannot but go this way. Then, your attitude must be different. You must be accustomed to eating humble food, being clad in poor clothing, being sheltered in tents and outdoors – you must know the taste of enjoying your life in this way. I began my work while you were not yet born. At your age I had accomplished much. But I thought there was a tremendous amount of work that I must accomplish during my lifetime. I knew that. I was never proud of my having done as much as I had. I was always anxious to accomplish more and more. I was in haste every moment. Do I look frustrated? Do I look tired? I am not tired. The farther I advance forward, the more strength is accumulated.

People think, "If I live this way or that, I will be happy." We think we are happy because we are living a certain kind of life. Then, who set up the standard? The definition of happiness – can it be right? You must say, "I did not set up the standard of happiness like that, so it has nothing to do with me. I have to create a new standard or definition of happiness." If you define happiness to be eating humble food, being clad in rags, being sheltered in a humble place, that is your standard of happiness for the time being. The people whose definition of happiness is like this will never fail in life – and in the end they can enjoy the utmost happiness.

Longer life on earth does not promise you happiness. Even though your life may be a brief one, if you have worked hard and have been recognized by God, upon entering the other world you will be welcomed and you will enjoy the flourishing and glorious life there. So, in this life, the question is how hard you work and how much wholesome fruit you produce. So, you must work at the risk of your life and at the cost of your life. If you go on like that you are sure to achieve victory. If you die without succeeding in your mission, God will be sorry, because He knows that you have been doing that at the risk of your life. Wouldn't God, in the position of Father, if He knows His son is going to die soon, want to give him something to help in any way possible? If you have that attitude, God is anxious and ready to help you. If you are confident enough to carry out 100 things, but you are qualified to carry out only 30, God is anxious to fill in the other 70. If you are doing this for your Father, wouldn't your Father be ready to help you? Our Father, with love, is, in a way, weak before His children. With love, He is ready to do anything you ask.

Then, what is the judgment of personality? If you are well-equipped, and you are the incarnation of God's Word, then you will be intact from Satanic invasion. Satan would attack you on the individual, family, national and worldwide levels. If you are attacked on the individual, family or national levels and you do not fall, you can advance more rapidly. If you are always on your toes, going forward all the time, when he beats upon you, the moment his hand is gone you will dash ahead with even more speed. So Satan will have to give up. Then he has to retreat and leave you. He will say, "However hard I try I cannot defeat this person." Are you like that? Would you want to be like that at least? If you want to be like that, can you accomplish it standing still? You must try hard. Satan will use on you the same cunning methods he has been using on our forefathers, past saints and martyrs. Now he is attacking you with that same power, but you must be more powerful and wiser. Then he will give up and leave you. After going through all these difficulties, when you attain the goal, God will find you there and will tell you, "Now I have found one who resembles me. You have gone through all trials and are here intact from Satan. As the victor, you resemble me, and you are my son." In that way you will pass the judgment of personality. That's the standard. God made everything a success, from the very beginning up to the present moment. If you resemble God, you will continue successes, and you must attain the goal and render glory to God.

You must have such a personality with which you can never fall prey to Satanic temptation. Before death, in the face of death, Jesus extended his arms and said, "Kill me," and at that instant he was not killed, and spiritually he was resurrected. If you are determined to lose your life for God, no Satan can kill you. You have eternal life there. Are you like that? If you are not like that, God cannot bless you. If He does, the blessing will be snatched away by Satan. But if you are so determined to face death without fear, then God will bless you and it cannot be taken by Satan. That is how to win in the judgment of personality. Win over all the temptations coming from Satan, and go to the standard where God can bless you. That's how it was with Jesus.

JUDGMENT OF HEART

The third judgment is that of heart or love. Have you ever loved a person in the true sense? Without that kind of love, you cannot be proud of yourself before God, before the past, present and future. You yourself must have loved to that extent.

The term "to love" means to love someone else in the object position. Love starts only when you have a person in the object position. What is the true standard of love? There are many kinds of love in the world: love between friends, between husband and wife, between parents and children. The question of love often brings a quarrel in the family. The wife may think her husband is loving her less than he used to, and that's the seed of the quarrel on her part. On the husband's side too his wife seems to be reserved in devotedness, and he is so greedy as to want utter devotion from her. Why is it so? It is because love should be unreserved. And if you are self-centered, if even a little bit of ego is there, we cannot call your love total. You must deny your whole being in loving your spouse. If a particle of you is left there, your love is not a wholesome one. Love must be like that. So if you find yourself self-centered, you must shake off that particle of yourself in your love.

How wonderful love must be if it is as pure as that. So true sacrifice [of oneself] must accompany true love. That sacrifice will be willing sacrifice. With this standard of love, you can win any individual, family, nation and the whole world. I must ask you again, have you ever loved a person with that kind of love? If not, you are not qualified to receive God's love. You cannot dream of receiving His love. Before wanting to have God's love, you must practice loving other people to that standard. You must long for not only your sweetheart, your lover, but you must miss every lost child of God with love of that kind. Until you are worn out in tears, until your legs are fatigued, until your whole energy is exhausted in search of that person, you must long for him. You must invest your life in that person; and your life will be multiplied in that person. You must plant your soul in that person and your heart will be multiplied. You must be loving people with that kind of love. Have you ever loved God with that kind of love? Without that kind of experience you cannot call yourself a whole human being.

In that case, you must be very humble and say to God, "I am not qualified for your love. Please don't come near me. I am not pure." If you are self-centered in love, you will just want to have God's love for yourself, and you would want to possess love of others. Then you are a robber of love. In order to love in the true sense, you must purify your love. As Jesus said, if your eyes would sin, if your nose, mouth, ears and limbs are used for impure love, you must feel like plucking them out or cutting them off. You must know that you are not qualified even to love the most unlovable man or woman. It is a very serious question.

I will become more serious. And you will have to cry. When I think of God, I am truly sympathetic with Him. Wholesome, perfect, absolute God always has to look at a world full of people who are spiritually disfigured, disabled, and crippled in heart. He is ready with beautiful, pure love to be poured down on us, but we are not ready to receive that kind of love. We are not ready vessels for the love to come. But He is ready to give us more and more love. Thus, He is a Being to be pitied. He has that pure kind of love for men; He is ready to save mankind despite all the hardships and disillusionment. For God to meet one man, the Messiah, to locate such a person as His true son, has been His desire throughout history. There have been multitudes of persons in the world who have been willing to receive God's love, but there has been no one ready to love God – except the Messiah. Our heavenly Father has been betrayed even by the many saints He has sent to the world, and by individuals, families and nations – by the whole of humankind, the whole world. His heart is aching and torn to pieces. We must restore Him to happiness. We must never cease to work until we return to Him with joy and happiness.

I would tell Him not to worry about anything. I am in His place to work for Him until the last one of all humanity has been turned back to Him. I feel that I am responsible for the totalization of all the betrayals committed by past humanity and all those saints who failed their missions. Thus, I have to return glory to God, to clear away His resentment and sorrow and disillusionment.

All through human history, God has been planting His love in human hearts, on the individual, family, national and world levels. God has never been able to reap all those loves; but we are here to reap, and by harvesting them we can return all He planted to God. You must be awakened to the fact that you are the totalization of the fruit of history. When you are harvested into God's hands, with all the rest of humanity, God gains your fruit. You must plant the heart of God into many people and have them multiply it to embrace the whole world.

How many people have you been loving with true love? Have you ever loved people with the heart of the Father, in the shoes of a servant, shedding tears for the people, sweat for the earth, and blood for heaven? Do you really understand what I mean?   You must ask yourself always, "Am I loving people with that kind of love?" With the love you have been receiving from God, you must go on loving all the rest of mankind. That's the heart of love. Unless you reach that standard, you are liable to the judgment of heart or love.

When you meet a person, you must think of the person like this, "I am here for this person." You must feel that what you have gone through, all difficulties and hardships, are for the sake of this person, will bear fruit in this person; and you will never let him go until he has returned to God. If you are in the position of absolute *plus,* then absolute *minus* will come about. So the question is always you, yourself. Have you ever awakened during the night, opened the window and looked out in meditation, thinking of your brothers and sisters, missing them and feeling compassion for them? Have you ever climbed up a mountain in the early morning and prayerfully looked down at the whole world and asked God to save it, feeling that you yourself were responsible for all mankind? You must be ready to help the people, save the people, and die for the people.

Are you qualified heirs to God? Can God rely on you, to leave everything in your hands?   That's the measure of love coming from God. It's a grave question. There is a set standard of love from God, and you must reach that point or go beyond it. Otherwise, you cannot come to God and embrace Him and call Him Father, and you cannot be received by Him. Unless you reach that standard, you are liable to judgment in the heart or love of God. Are you qualified to be received by God? He will wipe away your tears, your agony and the rest, and He will take you to the most sanctified place to change your clothes and give you all the glory He has. In the end, there will be a day in which the whole human family will be restored under God as the Parents.

The kingdom of heaven on earth is the dwelling place of those who have won in the judgment of heart. We will erect the heavenly kingdom on earth with our own hands. If we have that kind of love, God will come and abide in us and live among us. If every moment, in the process of loving, you feel that your love has not been enough, and if in repentance you want to have more love to be distributed to others, then the heavenly kingdom cannot but come through you. If you feel that your love is not enough, and you are tearful and struggle harder, then in the world of that kind of heart, the kingdom of God can come.

The Formula
for God's Providence

This evening I am going to talk about God's providence for mankind, how He began this providence and how He has been guiding it.

There must be a perfect goal for which all men are headed. There must be a goal, a final one, which God wants us to attain. If the desire of God and the desire of man differ, God's will can never be achieved. How to make those two, God's desire and man's desire, into one is the question. All people long for an ideal that is one, unique, unchangeable, and eternal. God, being absolute and the eternal Existence, wants the same thing. The crosspoint of those two, of God's will and man's wish, will be one point.

But what should it be? That is the problem. Neither man's desire nor God's will is ultimately human honor, human knowledge, material wealth, or human beings themselves. There must be some great goal that we are headed toward. That is the love through which God and man can unite into one and live together through eternity. Love is eternal. Those who love each other want to remain eternally in that love. Love is one. Love alone is the core of human desire. It must be unchanging.

Where would man want to meet God? What would be the first situation where man would want to meet God? We want to meet God as our Father and to have God meet us as His children. The situation where this is possible is the family. That is why we call God our Father and He calls us His children. When children have grown up, they marry. If a man and his wife are united, they build up the tradition of love among their family on the basis of their own experiences of receiving God's love. As husband and wife, they

43

are going to continue the tradition of the love which they have respectively experienced.

The individual receives love as a child, vertically, from God. Husband and wife have give and take of love horizontally. When they give birth to their children, their vertical love goes to them. In the love of their children a couple experience God's love for His children. With ourselves as the center, we receive God's love from above, vertically. Man and wife love each other, and they play the role of father and mother, giving love to their children. If that tie is unchanging and strong, God is right there in the family, and He will be always there. He will dwell with that family forever. If this kind of life had been realized in the beginning of history, there would have been no need of faith or prayer to believe in things that we cannot see or feel or touch. Our human ancestors were deprived of the pattern of how their families should have been.

I know you have learned about the human fall. We have no time to give a lecture on the fall. Due to the fall, however, we were deprived of those ideal families. Man was degraded from the original quality that was God's expectation. We are not the way God would want us to be.

We can live without material things. Even though we may lose the things we have, we can go on without them. We may be deprived of material wealth, family, friends, all these things, but still we can live on. But when we are robbed of love, we cannot live. In the Garden of Eden, when our ancestors fell, the most important thing that was lost was love. Love between God and man was lost. Due to the fall man lost three kinds of love: true parental love, true marital love, and true love of children.

We have not been able to receive God's true love as parental love. We have not experienced true love in the fullest sense between husband and wife. We have not experienced true love with our children centered on God. If that were the case, our children would be in the position of God's grandchildren. There are no people who have experienced these three types of love in the true sense.

Fallen man has never known what kind of love he lost, or what value that love really had. God, however, knew the value of those three kinds of love, and He was infinitely sorrowful because of the loss of love between Himself and man.

Let us imagine the first human couple, Adam and Eve. They were created as the true children of God; God was their Father. But due to the human fall, the love between them was cut off. Adam and Eve would have shed tears of joy when they fulfilled God's will. But instead they shed tears of sorrow in leaving God. It was a most miserable situation. Adam and Eve left God with no hope of return. Without this hope, how much greater their sorrow was. Imagine what fear they would have felt.

God foresaw their life of great difficulty. He felt there was almost no hope for Him to restore them. How great His sorrow was! For God, Adam and Eve were to have been His great son and daughter, but now they had been drawn away by the enemy Satan and had become Satan's children (John 8:44, Matt. 3:7, Matt. 12:34). God could not save them. God is the Center of man's love, life, and happiness, and man is the being without which God's purpose cannot be fulfilled.

God lost everything. Everything went to pieces. For men, too, every hope and happiness was lost. It was a very great tragedy; it was the saddest thing.

God was the Father. Would he not have the love which would not let His children go? He felt like forgiving them. But He could not do that. Therefore His pain was even greater. If there had been another son or daughter who had not fallen, and if this unfallen child could have asked God to save his brother and sister and give *him* their punishment instead, how would God have felt toward that third child? If there had been such a brother asking God to forgive Adam and Eve, God would have had a mind to forgive them. This heart of the heavenly Father became the basis for God's providence of salvation.

Suppose this third child of God's had gone to Satan and snatched his own brother and sister back to God's bosom. How would God have felt? Would He have punished them, or driven them out again or received them back? Would He have punished the brother who took them back? Would He have driven him out also? Or would He have praised him or left him alone?

If God would have praised him, then we cannot believe in the words of Jesus when he said, "Those who want to gain their lives will lose them, and those who are willing to lose their lives will gain them," (Matt. 10:39) and "Those who are first will be last, and the last will be first" (Matt. 19:30). He could not have promised that. Why? There are principles involved in taking back anything that is lost. It cannot just be snatched back. God cannot forgive man who rebelled against Him unless man himself sets up the conditions to come back to God, denying Satan. Originally, fallen man rejected God and went into Satan's bosom. So in return we must deny and reject Satan and come back to God's bosom all by ourselves. That is the condition.

Had the unfallen brother or anyone else gone to Satan and tried to take Adam and Eve back, Satan would not have let them go without a condition. In order to give up the fallen brother, Satan must be given something which he feels is more valuable than that which he is going to lose. In other words, there would have to be a man who is willing to sacrifice himself in place of his fallen brother. That sacrificial brother will become the second Adam, or Christ. The fallen brother will be liberated on that condition alone.

If there had been anyone who had had such filial piety toward God, His Father, that he could feel his Father's heart when He lost Adam and Eve, he would have felt that he would do absolutely anything to relieve the Father's grief and take back his brother. If that had been so, he would have been willing to sacrifice himself in place of his brother. When man fell, God was tearful. Both God and man were tearful when they parted from each other. Someone must come who will experience God's grief and his fallen brother's grief and who is willing to do anything to relieve those suffering hearts. The tears of that brother would not be the tears of sorrow. When man fell, God and man shed tears of sorrow. But these tears were shed for themselves. Another man must come who sheds tears not for himself but for God and his lost brother; they will be the tears of *hope*. With the coming of that man among mankind, there can be the hope of salvation. The gate of salvation will be opened with the tears which relieve God's sorrow and man's sorrow.

When you cry for yourself, your tears belong to Satan. As long as man sheds tears for himself alone, there can never be salvation. That is the problem.

We are taught about the problem of Cain and Abel in the Principle. To save Cain, there had to be Abel. Abel was in the position of the unfallen brother who asks God to forgive the fallen Adam and Eve because of him. To win that position, Abel had to first receive God's love. That means, he had to come out of the sphere dominated by Satan. Once he had won that separation from Satan, God could love him. Having gained that position, instead of being arrogant, Abel should have been willing to die for Cain. These three stages are the important formula: First, the man who is willing to save the world should be able to defeat Satan; then he must come into the love of God; and finally, feeling the heart of God and his fallen brother, he must be willing to sacrifice himself in place of his fallen brother, in order to relieve God's grief and his fallen brother's grief. Only on that condition can both be taken back to God. We know from studying the history of God's providence that Abel was killed by Cain while he was in the process of following that formula.

We see another example in Noah's act of building the ark on the mountain for 120 years – that long, long course of years while he fought against Satan. He must have been rejected by his wife, his family, his neighbors and relatives. From his nation and from the whole world, he received scorn and rejection. But if he had even once been tempted to not do what God had commanded him, he could have been claimed by Satan again. He overcame all difficulty and succeeded in carrying out his responsibility. God came to love Noah. But that is not all. When one comes into God's love, God sends him back into the world to be sacrificed, to be put into difficulties and suffer. This is in order to train him, of course, but also in order to save more people at the price of one who is willing to sacrifice himself. Noah, who was a righteous man, a just man, a good man, had to sacrifice himself for the sake of other people, not for himself.

Let us look at Abraham. God separated him from his father, the seller of idols. He had to leave his family, his native land, and his material wealth. God developed His providence to train him, to have him cry not only for his own nation, but for other nations, and even for the enemy. He did this by driving him away from the land of his forefathers, by sending him to other nations. He roamed about like a gypsy. He lived his life always with a prayerful heart and wishing God might save the people because of his prayer. That is why God blessed him with descendants as many as the stars in heaven and sand on earth. From the Bible we get the impression that God just blessed Abraham and loved him unconditionally. But this was not so. He had to cut himself off from his beloved family, his native land, his material possessions and go to the unknown land of God's choice, always feeling sorrow for God and the people. He prayed much for other nations. Only on that condition could God use Abraham as the father of faith and bless him so greatly. These things are not recorded in the Bible, but it was only because of such a background that God could bless Abraham.

Jacob went a similar course. He bought the birthright from his elder brother Esau. He left his home and went to the land of Haran where he worked for his uncle Laban as a slave for 21 years. His uncle had promised to give him his daughter Rachel as his wife. But after seven years, Laban deceived Jacob and gave him her sister Leah instead. If it had been you, you would have immediately spontaneously protested. But Jacob kept silent, worked for another seven years, and got Rachel. Then his uncle Laban deceived Jacob by trying to take away all the things that God had given him. Still Jacob did not complain.

Here we must know that even though Jacob was in the loneliest of situations, still he thought of nothing else but God's will. Because of that, other things in his life did not matter; the important thing was the accomplishment of God's will. Therefore he grew farther and farther from the world, but he came to receive more love from God. And after 21 years he won back all the blessed things he had earned and went back to Canaan. He knew his brother Esau was ready to kill him. Jacob, however, felt in his heart that all his wealth and accomplishment belonged to his elder brother. He wanted to give them all to Esau, all the things which he had earned with his sweat and blood. He prayed to God not to punish his elder brother Esau, and he asked God to bless him as He had blessed Jacob. Because of that heart, Esau was moved not to want to kill Jacob; and he too received God's blessing.

The same thing happened to Moses. Moses, after spending 40 years in Pharaoh's palace, had to leave all glory and wealth behind him, and cut himself off from the world. For the sake of his nation he was willing to sacrifice his life.

John the Baptist was led into the wilderness. He cut himself off from the past, and shed tears for the coming Messiah, for God, for his nation and his people. That is the point where he differed from the prophets previous to him. And when he prayed he shed tears of a different meaning. He shed tears for the nation; for the Messiah to come; and he cried for the sake of God. In that sense, he was the greatest of all prophets. In other words, the other prophets had no one whom they served as forerunner. John was making the way straight for the Messiah. The others did not pray for the ruler who was to come, but John did. That is the difference. But John prayed for the Messiah as the ruler of his own nation, while Jesus came as the ruler of the whole world. John's viewpoint was a little different from God's intention. That is the very beginning of his not being able to unite with Jesus.

He dreamed of the Messiah as coming to save Israel. He expected Jesus to observe the Mosaic Law, the system of the Israelites, but he found that Jesus was not doing that; in fact, Jesus appeared to be breaking the Law. Jesus was going to save the whole world; his scope was wider than and different from John's. There was no one nation in Jesus' sight. That is what made them different from one another. Thus John the Baptist stood on the side of the Israelites who opposed Jesus and caused his death. If he had stood on the side of Jesus and become one with him, he would have become Jesus' chief disciple, and John's disciples should also have become Jesus' followers. Then the whole nation, which believed John was the greatest of all the prophets, could have followed Jesus.

The chosen nation does not refer only to Israel, but to all those who separate themselves from evil and come into God's bosom. They are the chosen people. With those people as citizens, the chosen nation was to be formed. Jesus was to come among the separated people, among the people of God's choice. If the people had received Jesus, then he and the people would have formed a separate nation of faith, and the providence of salvation could have been extended to the whole of mankind. That separated nation had to shed tears to make themselves sacrifices for the sake of other fallen nations and for God, just as Abel should have done as an individual for others. But the people of Israel did not think in this way. They thought that Jesus would take the sovereignty of the nation, and under him they would lead happy lives, blessed with abundance both on the spiritual and physical levels. They desired all those things for themselves, not for others, and not for the whole world. It is God's will to send the Savior to the whole world, not just to one nation.

Israel could have established God's will. But the people didn't receive Jesus, so Jesus alone was determined to sacrifice himself for the nation and the world. Jesus had to leave his family, live in a solitary way, and receive God's love. Finally he made himself a sacrifice for other people just as the unfallen brother would have sacrificed himself for the salvation of fallen men and women. All people were in the position of fallen Adam and Eve. Jesus killed himself for them; he became the sacrifice. He did not curse those who killed him. He prayed and asked God to bless them. Therefore Jesus stood as the mediator between God and fallen mankind. He died as the unfallen Adam of the world. And he practiced the formula for the salvation of the people of the entire world. Therefore, he became the exemplary Adam. Whoever followed him received salvation.

From him a new world of salvation could be established. That is the history of Christianity. The church went through the same course as Jesus. Whenever Christianity went to a strange country for the first time, the missionaries who went with it had to undergo all kinds of difficulties and most were martyred. Those who died stood in the position where they could receive God's love and make themselves a sacrifice for others. If they had wanted to curse those who killed them, there could have been no providence of restoration. They had to pray for those who killed them. Without that kind of heart Christianity could never have proceeded.

The great people, the saints and holy men of the world have always separated themselves from the fallen world, from the world they belonged to, and have proclaimed or advocated something new. Then, at the sacrifice of themselves, they tried to influence or save all mankind. Always they longed for God. They have followed the course we have outlined. The four great sacred men of history were Jesus, Confucius, Buddha and Mohammed. Because they longed for God and for all mankind, they went through torture and persecution for all mankind.

A man might like his friends to sacrifice for him. If he follows his selfish purpose, however, there will no longer be friends around him; they will all go away. If that man denies himself and is willing to do things for his friends and sacrifice himself for the cause of greater value, it is natural that his friends would bring him also their relatives and acquaintances. The group would grow in number. God Himself would cooperate with such a group; He would be with such a group and for such a group.

In a limited sense, we might think the man was foolish to serve others and do things for others; but on the contrary, if one does that, he becomes a center around whom people will gather. Many more people would come to follow him and beg him to save them, lead them and control their lives. If the leaders of countries were that way, then their citizens would come to their knees before them, begging to be led by them. The individual, the group, or the world based on that formula must trust God, or all will diminish.

I want to teach you this: Love God and love people at the price of your life. Then you can gain your own life and gain all people also. That is what God wants from the bottom of His heart, and that is what Jesus wanted us to be like. When Jesus prayed at Gethsemane, "Father, let this cup pass from me, if it be possible. Nevertheless, not as I will, but as Thou wilt," his heart was that of a son who loved only his Father. On the cross he loved even his enemy and prayed for him. There had never been such a man in all history previous to him, and there was no such man after him. That is the sign of his having loved the whole of mankind. That is what made Jesus the greatest. If you can do that much, you cannot help but be the friend of Jesus, or the bride of Jesus. You can have his Father as your own. You can have everything he had.

Now, let us conclude. Those who shed tears for themselves are fools, great fools. Those who shed tears for others are wise men, because they can win God and win the whole world and everything in it. By doing that, you can be the possessor of God's love. You can hold the position of God's son and inherit parental love from God, true love between man and wife, and children's love. By possessing all these, you will be the richest of all people. You will stand in the position of having God's love, God's ideal, and man's purpose. Then you can embrace the whole world by love – true love.

In order to do that, you must remember the three stages of the formula: Separate yourself from Satan, come into the love of God, and sacrifice yourself for the sake of other people. In studying, you should not study for your own benefit or for your own sake, but you should study to save the whole world for God. When you marry, you must not forget that you are marrying for mankind, for the future of mankind. People with that heart cannot perish. When you pray, do not pray for yourself, but for others. If you do this the result will be yours also. Do not pray for the Unification Church, but pray that God may use you to save your nation and save the world, at the cost of your lives.

The place where such people meet, that is the Kingdom of heaven.

Heart

It is important for you to know about heart in order to love each other. "Heart" is a very difficult word to translate from Korean to English. What we mean has a deeper meaning than is conveyed by the English word. It means to be loving, caring, sensitive.

Heart is the source of love. God has an ideal within Him, just as we have an ideal we long for within our hearts. God's ideal can be realized through man. Then what is the vehicle through which man can express God's heart? In order for us to realize God's ideal, we were created masculine and feminine. Unless male and female beings come together and are united, there is no way for God to express His love ultimately. Unity is the measure of your love, and the source of joy in marriage. If you have your counterpart entirely one with you, working with you toward one goal, joy comes about. When you are happy, there is always you, the subject, and someone else, the object, with whom to share. In direct proportion to the degree of your love in being one with each other, your joy increases. The core of love in the true sense is something magnetic, and once you are united you can never be separated. So love means to be united internally and externally. Unless you find oneness, you cannot find joy. When you are one with a person, you don't want to be parted; you want to be with each other for eternity. You never tire of each other.

Which comes first, unity or love? You can love yourself when your mind and body are in harmony with each other. If you love yourself when your desire and actions are going different directions, then your love has little meaning. When your mind and body are united into one, then your love will be eternally protected by God. Unity is the beginning point of love the point where love can come to abide. This is God's ideal. Unless God can find persons whose quality is in accordance with His ideal, He cannot be happy at all. He has no one He can love.

Since this Principle is the core, we in our movement seek unity first And then we talk about heart and love. Then only can our ideal be realized Before the ideal can be realized, there must be unity, and then love.

When God created man, His ideal, Logos, was expressed in a male being and a female being; and in their unity, God's love was to be enjoyed by them To repeat: God's ideal exists. To fulfill it, unity must come about; then love will develop. When your two eyes are focused on one thing, your vision plays the proper role. If your eyes focus on two different things, you can't see anything at all. Likewise, when any subject and object are united to fulfill their function, love will be expressed there.

When you quarrel with a brother or sister, then God, as the Parent, cannot love either of you. If you have your own children, you will know this is true. As a leader of a group, would you love the members of your group when they fight with each other? Where there is harmony, there is beauty, and where there is beauty, love can come. In Matthew Chapter 5, in the Sermon on the Mount, Jesus said, "Blessed are the peacemakers, for they shall be called sons of God." Being sons of God means being loved by God.

When two fingers want to grasp something, they must come together. If two hands are clasped, the very deepest places in both are opened and joined together. When any two people love each other, they want to embrace, not turn their backs on each other. Remaining united is also the expression of love, so when you love each other, you will not separate from each other. If there is no love between you, you may come together anyway but you will be easily drawn apart. But where there is love, its magnetic power will keep you together. To be united means to be perfected in function.

Between nations, too, if any two nations are united, God's love will be there, and they will be blessed with good fortune in their partnership. There is an Oriental saying that where there is harmony in the family, everything can be done. Where there is unity and harmony, the love of God is present and the ideal can be realized there. In the ideal family, the husband and wife must be one. The children must become united with each other, brothers and sisters, and all together they will be in harmony like a symphony orchestra or a beautiful painting. With love there, no other power can intervene.

So we can come to the conclusion that if and when you want to receive God's love, you must be united. If that is done, you are already living in the Kingdom of God on earth. From there, the straight path to God is reached.

If anyone is asked whether he wants to receive God's love, he will answer in the affirmative. What should you be doing if you really want God's love? As an individual, your body and mind must be united. That is the basic thing. Then God's love will be with you. With that done, you can proceed on to be united with other people, and then the degree of God's love with you will be deeper and broader. Have you ever had the experience that your mind and body were entirely one in achieving some purpose? Have you thought it possible in the real sense? You try hard, but your thought and action are sometimes far apart, sometimes a little closer, and then they are separated again. The relationship between them zigzags all the time. There is a Korean saying that our mind fluctuates and vacillates from morning to night. "Mountains never change, but the human mind is always changing." So before wanting to be loved, you must have unity within yourself. In this world, everybody wants to be loved by others, without first trying to become one with them by understanding their hearts. No one can ever receive perfect love with that approach.

When you have made your mind and body united, then you have nothing to do with Satan. When your mind and body are one, you resemble God, so God will play the role of Subject to you, as a perfect object. Try to feel it. You must be able to feel God's love actually being with you when your mind and body are in harmony. When they are quarrelling with each other and you are divided within yourself, God will be far away.

If you can love one person, God's love will be there in proportion to the depth and size of that love. If you can love many people like this, God's love will come in proportion to the greatness of that love, to the depth of that love. Good people must be able to win others, not in such a way as to conquer them, but to love them, and to bring them into greater harmony and unity. Unity is the first thing you should desire. And if you love anyone at all, you should want to love him with your whole heart, even at the cost of your life. Then you can overcome hell. If you are not united, if there is disharmony, hell is there in your mind.

When you love someone, you always find that person is sacrificial toward you. There is already unity between you and that person. To bring that about requires sacrifice of individuality. Our purpose in uniting with others is to receive God's love. Then God's ideal will be realized.

Suppose there is a married couple, and they have some differences and distance between them. Would it be all right for the wife to take her position and call to her husband, "Come to me and you can become one with me," while the husband insists on his wife coming closer to him to be united with him while he stands solidly in his own position? That will never do. When you hold selfish love, then true oneness in God's love can never come about.

Then what is true love at all? This person does not have to go to the other to unite with him or vice versa, but both, when they come closer and closer can meet at one point between them. This can be true love. In other words, by both of them denying themselves, they can really unite with each other. And that is the standard of true love. Just one harmonious wholeness will be there. Love alone can make things round, harmonious, circular or spherical. In true love nothing can invade or interfere. Both parties must be obedient to each other, both must be willing to be united with each other. Together they will enjoy harmony and beauty. You may say, "Oh, no, I hate the word *obedience*. Why do I have to obey my husband or wife? I want to be freed from that bondage, and I want to be a free person." But in true love, obedience, loyalty, surrender – everything is possible, and you are not humiliated by it. You want to be controlled by your love.

In true love, then, there is a heavenly dictatorship of one to the other, and you want to live in this way throughout eternity. That is the intrinsic nature of love. You can be open about everything, let go of everything. This is glorious love, and the husband and wife do not think of themselves individually. Together, there is new meaning and significance. But that love doesn't originate from the man or the woman. It comes from no one else but God, the absolute Being of love, the highest dimension, the Source and Origin of love. And it can come only on the basis of unity.

The same theory can be applied beyond the family level. If there is unity among nations and the people of the world, then God's love will surely abound in that. Again I must say, there must be unity, and then God's love will appear. Then God's ideal will be realized. Not only among people is this true, but this principle applies also to the relationship between man and nature. To love nature is to become one with it. You must feel a closeness to nature. If you are the reflection of God's love, then nature is attracted to you. That love is the starting point of everything.

Suppose you want to write in a notebook. While you write, yourself and the notebook are one. If you love that notebook and pour out your whole soul and energy into it, then inspired writing can come out of it. You must have a strong feeling of this. Before you do anything, you must contemplate that thing and be sure you are one with it, or with that purpose. Then you can begin united in harmony, and the love of the work you are doing will be realized as the idea is actualized. In looking at things, you don't want to just vaguely gaze at things and see them with your eyes alone. If you focus your deep attention in looking at an object, you can penetrate into that object and it will become yours – you are in it and it is in you, in complete oneness. If your glance is focused fully on one point, from there it will broaden its scope, rather than just being cast about at random. When two meet at one point, they will go on together forever. Thus we can become aware of the world of spiritual dimension instead of this horizontal three-dimensional world alone.

If you meet another person and are united with each other, from then on something new is created. In that case, even though you are by yourself, you are not alone. Always you should live and act from a triangular base – God, your mind and body. Those three must be one. Your mind knowing and feeling that, senses that you are not alone. Then you are never lonely. Your body feels the same sensation. In that case, can you ever be dishonest, can you ever be false, when you realize God is always with you?

This is the whole nature of our conscience. When your mind is telling a lie, then your mind is cheating your body. Or when your body is disobeying your mind, then it means that you are also cheating God and cheating the creation, your parents, your brothers and sisters. Your mind and body being the core of your world, if those two are in strong oneness, you can become one with God, one with your parents, one with your whole family, one with your nation, and one with the whole world. If you are honest, you want to become one with each other and to unite your mind and body. If you are dishonest, you separate yourself, and you are destined to ruin.

This formula must be deeply rooted in your mind. Asleep or awake, whether you eat or study, you must always remember this. Then you are already receiving God's love. In order to be able to overcome unhappiness, you must be able to achieve unity. That's God's strategy to win the human heart. In order for you to win someone's heart, you must apply the same understanding.

When your mind and body are in perfect oneness, you can even hear your mind singing, and you feel light, as if you are flying or dancing. When you look at the world, it is so much more beautiful. It's as if you have eye-glasses of unity, and you are looking at things through God's eyes. Through those eyeglasses, everything in the world is beautiful. There is no ugliness.

Suppose the Son of God gave you a handkerchief. That handkerchief is worth more than gold, more than life, more than anything else in the world. If you are a real son of God, whatever the humble place you may lay yourself down, it is a palace. Then our clothing is no problem, and the place we sleep is no problem, because we are already rich. We are the princes of God. What kind of attitude must be created in ourselves? We will not feel hunger or thirst, difficulty or persecution, or anything which people in general may think hard to endure. On our way there is happiness, joy, and love. If you have God's love reflected in you, you want to reach out to every corner of the world, because God's mind is like that. If you have that attitude, the people around you will be attracted to you like iron filings to a magnet.

If you witness to people and you fail to convince them, it's not because God is not present, it's not because the people are evil, but it's because of yourself being without love. Then you must become a person capable of bringing unity. If you are united with someone, there will automatically come love, like air flowing into a vacuum. If your mind and body are really one, you feel God's love there like an electric current. Then you forget about fatigue, forget about hardship. You can experiment with living like that, and it will prove true. When you want to speak to the congregation, you want to have God speak through you. You must have your mind and body unified, or God cannot be with you. And before speaking to the people, you must repent if your mind and body are separate. Pray before God in repentance, shedding tears, and in deep prayer you must beg God's forgiveness, and then you can start talking. In that case you can be the spokesman of God. God may speak through you. The first step is for your mind to become one with God, and then your body will become one with your mind. In that case, God can work through you. Go on and try it, and it will prove true to you.

So you must have unity first, because without unity there is no love – unity first, love, and then God's ideal. You must think with God, say things with God, and plan things with God. The base of those three elements – unity, love, ideal – is heart. Heart is the deeper expression of the mind. Starting from heart, unity, love and ideal are all realized. We are told that everything starts from God. The core of oneself being heart, everything starts from there centered on God. Since our heart is the core, then God is the object to us. We seek Him. But in relationship to God's love, our heart is in the object position, receiving His love. When heart and God are put together, they love each other. We must know that the basic thing is our heart, our infinite heart. Creation came about from God's heart, a heart of love.

When those three are realized – unity, love, and the ideal – there is no distinction between the three. Unity is love, love is unity, the ideal is unity, the ideal is love. Then why are those three ultimately one? Unity came about on the horizontal level first. Two elements are one, and then God's love can dwell there. In this way we have a vertical relationship, also. Love will be the director of the three. Then the ideal can be fulfilled.

To repeat this, there must be unity on the horizontal level between the two. Then God can become one with that unit. You can have both a horizontal relationship and a vertical relationship, and those three will be put together with perfect love. They will be in ideal harmony throughout all eternity. When you dance around in joy together, you don't make a distinction between your place and your partner's position. There is no distinction between you. You can stand in his position, and he can stand in your position. There is unity, love, and your ideal.

But knowing this alone cannot do anything. If you really understand, put it into practice.

When you say about anything, "This is mine," you must love that thing and must be able to realize your ideal through it. If those three are accomplished in you, you cannot be anything else other than a citizen of the Kingdom of Heaven. Is that clear to you? You must always be thinking of unity, unity, unity. When you see, see unity. Eat unity, smell unity, hear unity. Everything must be unity first, and then love and harmony, and then the ideal.

America in God's Providence

The history of humankind has had no clear goal or motive. From the viewpoint of today's situation, there is a serious question: Do we live in the form of the ideal world, or will the ideal world emerge from an extension of the present world?

More and more people long for one ideal world with freedom and peace, and we can readily understand that longing. But by the trend of the present world, we can never reach the world which all people desire. Therefore, our present goal is very indefinite and unclear.

Can we find any one nation which can take the responsibility to build such an ideal world? I think most people living now in the United States cannot lead this world to fulfill such a hope, nor is there anyone in the Communist world who can do so. America has not found the ideal which will make people love the world more than their own country. The present United States, therefore, cannot be the nation to lead us to the ideal world. Likewise, the Soviet Union in the Communist world cannot be the country to establish such an ideal world. There will be no prosperous world, or peaceful world until the American people and the Soviet people can sacrifice themselves for the benefit of all mankind and the whole world, but there is at present nothing leading them to do so.

All things are developing from some cause. Now, this world is not the world all mankind desire. Therefore, in the beginning there must have been something wrong. In other words, history started from a wrong motive. We must correct this to achieve the goal of God and man. The goal cannot be reached simply by correcting the various problems in this world of result; we must go back to the starting point and correct the original motive.

Was the world created from a unified motive? We find that nations are not unified, and races and families are not unified. And even the world is divided into blocs. In nations there are opposing parties. In homes there are divisions among members, and within the individual, mind and body are divided. The question is: Why is the world divided? What is the cause which brought the whole world, nations, families, and individuals into conflict?

God is absolute. If all individuals and the whole world were made one with this eternal Cause, then how could such a divided world exist? We have to deduce that this absolute God was not involved in forming the divided world.

If the world is to be unified, someone must destroy all the problems that were caused by evil. That is the mission of religion. Whoever is looking for the ideal world must investigate the cause and destroy evil. To find the root of evil is most important. If we can't find it, we can't restore the world. By finding the evil cause in ourselves we can solve all the problems of the individual. The important thing is to find one person who has become one with God, who has a mind and body which do not struggle with each other, centered on God. Therefore, the most important goal is not solving all the problems of the world, but to find the self that is not divided and struggling against itself. If God exists, He must show us the way to restore our original state. He must teach us to become ideal individuals.

Therefore, through the course of history, God designed His providence to call one such person from among mankind. Man lives in his home with his family. Also he lives in the material world and in his nation. For God to restore His nation, His family, His individuals, and His material world, He cannot simply take these things back from evil without any condition. The evil possessor would try to retain all these things. Therefore, the direction of good and evil must be different. If one goes to the right, the other one goes to the left. All people want to have a unified world, but this cannot be obtained easily.

You are in the central position in the struggle between good and evil. It is not easy for you to know which is more serious – the fall of a nation or the the fall of an individual. For man, the most important thing would be his own demise. We have a tendency to want not to sacrifice ourselves for others. Everyone has a mind to make all things center on himself. So to reach the world which we long for and desire, we have to overcome obstacles which stand in our way.

If we make one world by conquering other nations, we will never have a peaceful or happy world. We cannot have such a world by fighting others.

Because God knows this, He goes the opposite way. In this world there are two ways of life. Evil wants to make one world by beating others, but God chooses a different way.

The degradation of mankind, the fall of man, came from the attitude that one would be willing to sacrifice others for his own benefit. As you know, the cause of evil was the Archangel who, for his own enjoyment and benefit, sacrificed Eve and Adam. As Adam and Eve were the ancestors of all mankind, he sacrificed the seed of mankind for his own personal benefit. The world has developed according to that pattern, from the evil motive. The Archangel, to fulfill his desire, sacrificed others even though his desire was false. Likewise, rulers throughout history have sacrificed other people for their own causes. The strong have had the dominating power. Struggle began between individuals, spread to the struggle between families, to the struggle between tribes, nations, and even worlds. Today there is no peace and no ideal world.

Now history is at the stage when the two blocs which have tried to sacrifice each other are tired. The democratic nations want to make one world but have almost given up. The Communist world wants to dominate the whole world, but it has also come to this position. Therefore, this world cannot now be unified by either the democratic world or the Communist world. How this world can in fact be unified is a very serious question.

All people want to have a peaceful, happy world. But we are in despair; we cannot find the way to the unified ideal world. Before mankind is a big obstacle. We cannot pass the obstacle if we put our own national interest in the first place. We can achieve the ideal world only with the thought that to achieve the ideal world we are willing to sacrifice our own nation. With such thoughts alone can we continue and overcome the obstacle before us.

The reason for the conflict between Soviet Russia and China is that Russia wanted to make the Communist world center around herself, while Red China wanted to make it center on China's people. The United States is the leading country in the democratic world, but she has not been able to fulfill that role when she thought of her own interests more than those of other nations. America and Russia seem ready today to throw away the whole world to save themselves. There must be one nation who can sacrifice herself for the establishment of the ideal world. When we find such a nation, we can have hope for one ideal world. That nation does not exist for her own benefit, but for the sake of the world.

The purpose of God is contrary to the purpose of evil. As God's providence was thwarted in the beginning, we have the directionlessness of the present world as a result. God has gone the course of teaching religious people. First He had to find one individual on His side, completely one with Him – who could not be broken away from Him. And this man must come to the position where he can make one unified world. Therefore the primary intention of God is to find someone to become one with Him. And his teachings must be to love God and to sacrifice oneself for the world. Because man is in the position which is derived from the evil cause, as he is he cannot go to God. He must reverse his direction. To love God, man must abandon his world, his family, material things, and even his own life. Then when he really loves God, God must love him. That man, as the one who receives God's love, must sacrifice himself for the world. That is most important; that is the core of God's providence.

When we think about the words of God that we must love Him with all our hearts, all our minds, all our spirits and everything we have, we might think God is like a dictator. But all these commandments are not for Himself. When we love Him with all our hearts and all we have, He will love us just as we love Him. That was God's intention and His first commandment to us. Therefore, the word "love" is absolute. When we love Him, He loves back. The command which asks for us to love Him with all our beings means to love Him with our life by sacrificing ourselves. For God to love others, He must sacrifice the one whom He loves the most. Because of such teachings, we call God love. Because God sacrificed those whom He loved most for the world, God is the greatest Love.

Among the world religions, therefore, Christianity is the one central to God's purpose because Jesus Christ gave himself as a sacrifice for others. More than that, he even prayed for his enemies to be blessed by God. The spirit of Jesus was to be an offering for others. Following his pattern, many Christians have been martyred for God's cause. Families have been sacrificed, and tribes and nations were given up for the sake of God. So for the providence of God to come to the worldwide level, God is demanding that one nation come forth and sacrifice herself for the blessing of all mankind. God needs such a nation to represent the world.

Can we find such a nation on this earth? There is no such nation sacrificing itself. Therefore religion must sacrifice itself for a nation, and that nation must sacrifice itself for the sake of the world. Then the world must sacrifice itself for the sake of God. That way God's ideal of one world can be reached. Religion in America must sacrifice all that it has to save America. That religion should not fight to multiply itself but should work to save the nation, sacrificing its own churches. If it works with such spirit, then that nation will eventually unite with that religion. When this religion and its nation unite they will go forward to save the whole world, sacrificing themselves.

For that position, the United States is the representative nation of the democratic world. God purposed the United States to fulfill the mission of the sacrificial nation. Therefore, God sent to this land the Pilgrims, who risked everything and made such a great country in such a short period of time. When the Pilgrims came to this country, they built first churches, then schools, and finally they built their own houses. The backbone of America's prosperity, the root of the development of the United States into a great nation, is the spirit which puts greater stress on the public purpose than the private purpose.

God is looking for the representative country through which He will inherit the world. To become greater, we must give to those less than we are. When the United States gives greater aid to other countries, she will receive more respect. But as she decreases what she gives, she loses that respect and becomes isolated from other nations. If, in spite of her own difficulties, the United States continued to give foreign aid and directed the giving out of this aid to her fellow democratic countries even to a sacrificial degree, then what would happen? If the United States became weaker by such a giving-out policy, then all the other countries would become sympathetic to the United States and would defend and support her, come what may.

Why has Christianity spread all over the world? Because Jesus' sacrificial spirit is in the heart of God's providence. It is the basic spirit of God's providence to make oneself a sacrifice for others. Christianity has received much persecution, but the more it received persecution, the more it prospered. Jesus did not leave behind any well-reasoned philosophy like Marxism, but by the spirit alone he produced such a great effect in the world. That was done not only by Jesus himself, but by the providence of God and by the cooperation and will of God Himself. Therefore, the most important thing for any nation is that she sacrifice all things for the world and all mankind. From such a nation will come out a system developed from Jesus himself. The future ideal world will begin from there. That nation will sacrifice her sovereignty for the benefit of the whole world.

The United States is far away from this position. The individual and individualism are good in balance, but if too much stress is put upon that way of thinking, everything collective and virtuous is lost – the love of the nation, the brotherhood of the people, the family integrity, the relationship between parents and children – and finally even the value of individuals themselves. If all things are levelled, you become like hawks and blow where the wind blows. That is the reason there is no peace.

For America to stand in accordance with the providence of God, there must be a new movement in America. Americans as individuals and America as a nation must follow the spirit of God and the truth of Jesus Christ and make this nation a foundation for the expression of God's ideal.

Where do we find such a new movement of spirit? I think there are many churches in America vacant or just attended by old people. There is no fire and no traditional spirit. That means that God has left these churches, and Jesus Christ has abandoned them. Through these churches the providence of God cannot be dispersed. The church must find individuals that will sacrifice themselves for their families, sacrifice their families for the American nation, and sacrifice the United States for the world. The ideal that can lead the whole world must come from the spirit of sacrifice for the greater cause. For the benefit of the whole world, one nation must really give herself to pursue the one ideal world.

Where can we find such a nation, such a family, such an individual? We cannot find anyone like this. Therefore these are the Last Days. The end has come to the world. The end has come to the church, nation, tribe, and individual. This is the end of the world.

We have to understand clearly our role. The Unification Church was formed to develop the providence of God. The spirit of the Unification Church is first to sacrifice the individual to find the family. We sacrifice the family to find other families; to find the nation we sacrifice the tribe; and to find God's world we sacrifice the nation. This is the role of our church. We are not sacrificing all these things for the benefit of the Unification Church, but we are sacrificing ourselves for the benefit of the whole nation, and for other churches.

I want to give you an example. Let's say a man has ten friends. If this man goes to his friends every day and asks them to do something for him, the friends will do so one time or two times, but then they will go away. They won't even say goodbye. But if this man serves all his friends, sacrificing himself, doing something for them, then the friends will stay with him and will even bring their friends and families to him also. If this man wanted to leave, his friends would cling to him and ask him not to go. In the first case, everyone is leaving him; therefore, that man will come to unhappiness and destruction. In the second case, however, everyone comes to him; therefore he will prosper and grow.

Good and evil are fundamentally different. Evil asks everything and everyone for itself. It asks everyone to be and exist for himself. But good lives for others. The way to destruction is to conquer others; the way to prosperity is to serve others. We have to understand that this is the dividing point. When we follow the formula of good, we become the greatest people. But if we go the other way, we become dictators. The saints are those who sacrificed themselves for the sake of mankind and God.

We revere four great religious men – Jesus Christ, Confucius, Buddha, and Mohammed. Those are the ones who lived for God. They did not live for themselves, or for just their own nations, but for the whole world. Therefore, they were persecuted by their own people and nations. Those four saints are the founders of the major religions. These are the historical facts; they cannot be changed. But now, the people of this modern world even deny religion, saying that religion has nothing to do with the world. Religions are the symbols of morality and discipline, but the world today tends to reject them. Without religion, however, this world can never restore itself.

The Communists are entirely opposed to this view. According to Communist ideology, "Mine is mine, and yours is mine" [all things belong to the state]. For that reason, we can predict that Communism will not last long. To achieve their goal, the Communists never choose the least or the smallest, but the greatest and largest for themselves. On our parts, we must think, "Mine is yours, and yours is the nation's, and the nation's is the world's, and the world's is God's – and God's is mine." If we become people like that, then God will want to give His heart to us.

We believe that everything can belong to God. You and your house and your family can be occupied by Him eternally. The size of the country does not matter. What God needs is this: to find before Satan His faithful son, His faithful family, and His faithful nation. He wants to know that because such a nation exists, evil can no longer dominate the world.

God is the God who has no nation which He can love. God is the One who has no family, no tribe, no individual whom He can love. Two thousand years ago, God sought such an individual, Jesus Christ. With him, with the tribe of the Israelites, and with the nation of Judah, He wished to establish a nation He could love. But that nation looked after its own benefits, rather than seeking the good of the whole world. Therefore, the providence of God was spent, and He couldn't complete the restoration through His son. The people of Israel were devout believers in God. But they didn't think about God's will more than their own individual things, their own family things, their own tribal things, and their own national things. That's the reason why they could not understand Jesus.

By the crucifixion of Jesus, God lost His chosen people. To take their place, Jesus established spiritual Israel, Christianity (Romans 9: 6-9). Christians are today in the position of Israel, the nation of faith which should have received Jesus Christ. There is no one nation in Christianity. Therefore, when the Lord comes again, the pattern will go the same way as it did when Jesus was rejected (Luke 18:8). God chose America as a nation playing the role of John the Baptist, and also the churches in America to play the role of preparing the way for the Lord to come. But America and her churches are thinking of their own benefits more than God's purpose. From God's view-point, if America cannot fulfill her mission, God must search for another nation.

So all the members of the Unification Church must sacrifice themselves, their families, their friends, and even the Unification Church itself, to establish such a nation which God can love. The present problem is whether we can act as saints in our daily lives – that is the most important thing.

America has been the most advanced country in the world. If America cannot fulfill her responsibility to love the world at the cost of herself, then America cannot stay in the position of the leading country. We desire to create model individuals, model families and model tribes which will serve as a pattern for the rest of the world.

God is the Parent of mankind so He feels most sympathy and love for those people who are suffering in poverty and distress. In our families, parents feel much more concern and love for the smaller, weaker child than they do for the one who is very capable. God feels the same way.

When a movement with His attitude arises in America, then America will help the underdeveloped countries. Then this country can remain the leading nation. Our members of the Unification Church must always bear in mind when they sleep in a comfortable place that faithful workers for God are sleeping in a worse place; when they eat delicious food they must remember that more hard-working brothers and sisters are eating poor food or have none at all. We must think that we have to raise living standards for all.

When one friend serves ten friends, they will come to him as the leader in service. Likewise, when one nation serves others, they will desire to have that country as their leader. In order for America to endure and prosper, there is no other way than for her to give out her blessings.

Everything goes in cycles. After spring, summer comes; after summer, autumn comes; then winter; then spring; then summer and autumn again. If you go up, you must be prepared to come down. Man cannot go up and up forever. Everything, everything, comes around. So after one has gone to the top, one must know how to come down again.

America must go to the underdeveloped countries and the underdeveloped countries must follow America. In that way the whole world can survive and be united, even eternally. In the center of that unity, God dwells. Then one peaceful, ideal world can exist.

Children of the Heavenly Father

Because of the human fall, we have not seen God in the true sense. We have not had the true God, in a way. We have not been living with the true God. If we as mankind could have been one with God, with God as our Father, abiding in Him, living with Him in the greatest love, how happy we would have been! And on God's part, how happy He would have been to live with His true children. He, being the Highest in every sense, could have been overjoyed, with unimaginable happiness. He would have lived with us in the ultimate love. Have you ever stopped to imagine how He would have smiled and danced and been delighted to see us? It is our great loss not to have been able to live with such a Father, from whom everything good and happy starts. But we have never experienced such a sensation to the fullest degree.

We experience the love of parents over us. Our parents kiss us on the cheek, embrace us and console us in times of sadness. We have experienced these things but not to the full extent, and not in the true sense, because every sensation can come in its fullest degree only from God. What we have experienced in the world apart from God is not from God, but dominated by Satan. Have you ever stopped to think who it was who made the first smile in the whole world, the first laughter in the whole world? Of course, there were Adam and Eve, who could have been joyful if it were not for the fall, but who was the one to be joyful at the time of the human fall? Satan. Not God. Satan was happy after he took away God's sovereignty over man and was able to have all mankind under his dominion. The smile of Satan, the laughter of Satan was horrible when he took control of man. Following the fall, history proceeded for the most part in accordance with Satan's will. Our forefathers worked and did things in such a way that they pleased Satan more often than they pleased God.

If you really felt that, if you seriously considered that horrible reality, you would be almost choked by it. You would want to abandon this world, to fly away to another world. Do we have an inch of land that we can claim as our own, as God's children, where we can be joyful and happy? We don't have such a place. Though we might want to leave this earth, we have to restore it to its original condition.

If we leave the world as it is, we may as well hope that God will not come and abide in this world with us. You should feel like stopping Him from coming to this dark world. If you are really the children of God, you will feel that way, because everything is opposite from His desire.

God, however, on His part, always wanted to come and abide with us, helping us, saving us, but we men of sin, we children of disobedience, have prevented God from loving us and living with us. How sad God's heart has been! If there were a single man, who in the place of all mankind would sacrifice himself to save the world, to erase the sin of other people, desiring to be a victim for the sake of God, would God be pleased with him or not? In that case, would He have rejected that man or said to him, "You are one of them; you are a stained, sinful man. I don't like to look at you. I don't want you to help me in any way"? Would God have said a thing like that? As lofty and pure as God may be, He needs someone to help Him in His restoring the world. So God would be grateful to have found that kind of man, and He would ask that man to do certain things for Him. But to find such a man has been very difficult.

What if that man would say to God, "I've sacrificed myself for your cause; you must recognize me," insisting that God would acknowledge him? How would God feel? Man is so greedy. We want to have things more than we have earned. But if that person of central mission were thinking that way, saying those things to God, if I were God, I would tell him, "Oh, now you have proven that you are also of the Satanic tribe. I don't want to have you." God must have felt that way toward such people.

Don't you remember, when Jesus prayed in Gethsemane, "If it be possible, if it be possible, let this bitter cup pass from me. Nevertheless, not as I will but as thou wilt." If Jesus had not included in his prayer, "Not as I will but as thou wilt," God could never have accepted him. That is the secret of being God's son. It is to be utterly obedient to God's will. Only in this way can you make God happy.

In the world of evil, there is only one road for God to go. That's the road of sacrifice made by the man of sin who is willing to get rid of whatever he has in order to receive God. How do you feel after hearing that? Sad, serious? You are here ready to receive God, but God wants you to sacrifice yourself even before being told to do so. That's what kind of person God would want you to be, because He wants you to surpass the standard of fallen men. Because of that His heart is sad. Unless you are ready to sacrifice yourself before you are told to do it, God cannot come to you. If you live like that, God will be proud of you before Satan. Unless we do that, there is no way for us to restore God's authority and dignity as His children.

You must make a hopeful prayer to God, "Oh, Father, I don't want to be a foolish child, to be unwise. I want to know your heart. I am here ready to sacrifice myself, so why don't you come and abide with me." For that prayer, God will be proud of you.

And you can even pray this: "Father, I will be responsible to restore this world, and I can do it, believe me. You don't have to come and help me. I don't want you to come to this world of suffering to help me. You stay there and watch me." With that kind of prayer you can console God's heart. Then how would God respond? He would tell you, "I am coming. I must come and help you. Even if you want to stop me from coming, I have to be with you. I want to be with you, right in the midst of darkness." God would say that to you. Then when you are pursuing your mission, ready to fight your way through all difficulties, you will suddenly find that God is already there before you, having prepared everything for you and paved the way ahead of you.

God is the God of love, of parental heart. In that case, if you were God, wouldn't you do the same for your children? When you live like that with God, you become the greatest of His sons, since you have moved your Parent's heart. You will have restored God's dignity, and He will be proud of you.

I have thought and thought and finally found that this is the only way for the sons of filial piety to please God. You will be grateful that God has come to earth because of you. You will be able to make God happy, warm and proud. And you will be proud of each other and satisfied with yourselves.

I imagine all of you pray hard. Hungry or full, satisfied or dissatisfied, you are always praying hard to God. But the degree of your fervor will decide how much your prayers will be answered. In praying, too, your attitudes will differ from one another.

I am sure, when you pray to God, there are some who are confident that their prayers will be answered. But some of you think, "I want to do so much for Him, but first He has to answer my prayer." God would not want you to change the way you are praying just to suit Him. However, He would

want to have you pray harder and more earnestly. When you pray, it is something like this: Suppose that God is looking in this direction, and your voice
comes praying so hard and diligently. His concern will be drawn to answer
your prayer. God is looking closely at every one of you, and He will find
that someone without even praying is doing things in such a way that his
prayer is already answered. Then God's attention will be drawn to that
person.

If He has two children, and one is praying so hard even though he was
not told to pray, and the other is only reluctantly praying after being told, to
whom would God be drawn? I don't think there is anyone among you who
does not know the answer.

Suppose there is one child who would nod to his father after being told
to do something. But there is another child who on his own initiative has already found out something and would come to his father and ask whether or
not what he had discovered was true. Which of the two would delight the
father more? Again, one child may be aware of what is happening around his
father, but another child is so anxious to become involved in his father's
world that the first thing in the morning the child would think, "Is Father
up? What are his plans for today?" To which would the father's heart be
drawn?

There may be still another child who can't help but wake his father up
because he has thoughts of some wonderful plans himself. He would knock
at his father's door or just rush into his room and wake him. But the father
would still love that child.

If you were in the position of the father, would you love a child who
just clings to you for 24 hours without even letting you sleep? If you are loving and concerned about your father, even if you irritate him and even if you
prevent him from doing anything else, he is forced to be concerned with you
and love you in return. The same thing is true with God, our heavenly
Father.

I am going to tell you a story about my son, Hyojin. He is a very active
boy. He runs so fast that he trips over things. One day he fell and skinned
his legs, and I found them swollen and bleeding. He was such a tiny boy. I
asked him, "Does it hurt you?" He was bleeding, but he told me, "It doesn't
hurt. I'm all right." I have never forgotten that scene. Instead of crying, the
boy comforted his father.

Among God's children who are working hardest there are two kinds.
Some would want to serve God because they are anxious to be loved by Him.
They are contented and satisfied to enjoy the Father's love. But other children are worried about their Father's cause and know He is eager to reach out
and find other children. Such a person would tell God that since He has lost

so many children, he wants to bring them back to Him. Would you say, "Father, wait for me. Even though I may be away from you doing this work for a while, don't worry about me"? If you went out in search of your lost brothers and worked very hard and didn't return to your Father for a long period, would your Father be discontented with you? It is clear that God would love you more if you are the child who would want to go out in search of the lost brothers and sisters and bring them home.

Suppose the child working to restore the lost children would even die at the front-line, would the Father be angry because His son had disobeyed Him? He would be so proud of him. He would cherish the heart of that child and love him all the more. So you should do things without being told to do them and without complaint. You must be more serious than He is about carrying out what He has in mind.

The Father's love and patience are with the child who is always ready to help Him in any way possible, and who would go anywhere for the sake of the great task to be carried out. He would long to have that son around to take care of His children and great-grandchildren. In that way His love would be multiplied through this person.

There are various types of heart. Some fathers would tell their children, "You must love me and no one else, and you must serve me and no one else – because I am your father." But there are other fathers who would tell their sons, "Instead of loving me and doing things like this for me, why don't you go around and do things for others, because I love them as much as I do you." That kind of father is the real father. When you are unwilling to sacrifice yourself, if this father would drive you out even to death for the sake of his many other children, that father is the true father.

After you have finished your work here on earth, when you go to the next world, if you tell God that you would not want to go to Heaven but would stay in hell to help the people there, then God would bring Heaven down to you for you to live in. Don't you think He would do that? Then if you would insist on His letting you live in the lowest society, He would smile and say to you, "Son, you are a very smart boy." In that case, even though you were not obedient to God, He would still be proud of you. You would be an example of utter goodness.

He would tell you someday, "You don't have to go out to society. When did I tell you you had to go out and witness to the people? Why don't you stay here and rest? " If you would object and protest and finally go out to society, would He punish you? God, in trying to save the whole of mankind, would want you to have this attitude. He would want you to desire to be this kind of Christian.

That's why in the Bible we read many paradoxical things. In one place you are taught to love your Father with all your heart, all your might, all your sincerity. That's the first commandment of God. Later we are told to love our neighbors as ourselves. Taken together, these commands seem paradoxical, but if they both are carried out, you can win the whole world.

When God tells you to love Him more than anyone else, it means that He wants you to carry out His will at all costs. So it is natural for you to love your neighbors and to love your brothers and sisters as you would yourself. If you are to resemble your Father, would you love just one person who will satisfy your personal aims, or would you love all the people of the world for His sake? God loves the great combination of all people – including the people of the past and future generations. The broader the scope of your battle is, the more you are loved by the heavenly Father.

If you want to come to the position to be loved by your Father, your relationship to the world will change. Suppose you pass by the scene of an accident where someone has been injured. You would feel so sympathetic, as though that person were someone very near to you, and you would like to help him in any way possible. You would want to tell the people standing around also to be sympathetic. If the other bystanders are only watching and doing nothing, you would be so anxious, as if that person were your own child. You would put him into your car and rush him to the hospital yourself.

Or you may meet a wonderful person who is accomplishing great things in the world. You would want to talk with him and encourage him. You would be grateful to God that you had met such a good person, and you would want to be associated with that person and get to know him heart-to-heart. You would feel like placing yourself in the position of the parent to that person, and you would want to endure for him; you would pray to God that what he had done would be received by Him, that his sins and the sins of his ancestors would be forgiven. You would feel one in heart with him, in joy and in sorrow.

You should love the world in such a way that you would ask God to bless a prosperous country all the more and guide it to become the leading nation of the world: "I want to see you being joyful over this prosperous country after having poured out so many blessings here." On the other hand, if you see a poor people in an underdeveloped and underprivileged nation, you should feel the zeal swelling up in your heart to make that nation see the sunshine some day. You would want to elevate the standard of living in that nation, because you hate to see your Father in anguish over the suffering in that nation. You would be eager to make it equal to other nations. You would desire these things without reservation.

Then, what must our desire be? Our desire is to become the children of

God, doing everything in His place before His orders. Our desire is to become the kind of people the sinful history of mankind has never seen before.

Would God want you to laugh and be happy before He made you happy? If you have had the experience of raising children, you know the answer well. Suppose a father and mother quarrel with each other and are so unhappy, never laughing or smiling. They are in a terrible mood, but their children, innocent ones, would come to them, smiling, laughing and dancing about trying to make their parents laugh. Wouldn't they laugh? Even though you may want to stay in a bad mood, to remain angry, when you look at your children who are trying to make you happy, your heart will burst into laughter.

Which is better — to have your children unhappy and to try to soothe their hearts, even when they are sad because they know you are burdened, or to have your children want to make you happy? Wouldn't you like to have children who will try to cheer you up? Our desire is to become that sort of children to God.

In order to be that way, first, you must be doing things before you are ordered to. Second, you must be so aggressive that you want to act by yourself, even without the help of your Father. You will tell Him: "Father, please stay where you are. I will be responsible. I will do my part. Please wait until I can return this accomplishment to you. I am doing this for your sake and for the sake of my brothers and sisters whom you love dearly." The third thing is, as I just said, you must desire to do things for the sake of your brothers and sisters all over the world because they are equally loved by God. If you feel that way, you are His restored children whom God loves the most. He would praise you, and He would like to give you anything. He would be proud of you.

When He gives praise and everything good, you may say: "Father, now that you have given all this happiness and these blessings to me, they are mine, aren't they? " He would tell you, "Of course they are yours." Then you can do anything you like with them. You would want to give all your blessings out to other people, thinking, "Let all that I have received belong to my brothers." God would be happy with you.

If you do this, you will be the sons and daughters of filial piety to God. He lost His love, His happiness, His peace and His whole creation because of the human fall. Therefore, you will want to return to Him through others the absolute happiness, love, and ideal He has given you.

If you take that position, you can attract the heart of the heavenly Father. You can have the true love of God in your possession, and that is the core of everything. If He found that kind of son empty-handed after having given out all that he had, the Father would tell him, "I am yours. You can have me." With this in mind, you can interpret the whole Bible.

If you would walk your path in this manner, God will turn to you to be with you. You can meet Him wherever you are. However low the place where you are situated, your Father's attention will be focused on you there. The kingdom of God in which He takes delight will be right there in your heart wherever you are.

You must be keenly aware of the fact that you are not born for yourself. You are born for the sake of the whole world; you are living for the sake of the whole world; you are ready to die for the sake of the whole world. If you live this idea to the fullest extent, then you will already be carrying out what your Father wants you to do. Then the whole creation will want to belong to you, and God Himself will be yours. Even if you didn't want them, all things would volunteer to come to you and belong to you.

When you feel, "I am born out of my Father, and I am already a part of Him, and I want to be with Him and do everything for Him forever," then you are already in the position to be loved by Him and to inherit from Him. Even when you die, you know that you will live in the other world in spirit, and He will love you all the more.

Then what would you lack?

If you are in that position to be always with your Father in spirit, then you are going to live with Him wherever you are, all through eternity. So asleep or awake, whatever you are doing, don't ever think that you are alone. You are always with your Father, and your Father is always with you.

God's True Nation

In the history of every nation there is rise and fall. Sometimes a nation reaches a peak of its culture, and sometimes it declines. Everyone wants to be proud of his own nation, his own culture or tradition. But are even those high points of culture up to the standard that we can be proud of throughout all eternity and before all humanity?

The world as a whole is not the ideal place to live in or to want to be proud of. If God exists, we can certainly say that this world is not the ideal world in which God intended us to live. We know that God is the ultimate, absolute Being, and His standard must be the same. Then, are we pleasing God by our thoughts and actions? There are smiles and laughter in the world, but since the fall of man these smiles and laughter have not really pleased God. Whether you are happy or sad, experiencing success or failure in life – does what you are doing have anything to do with God's providence? To reach the ultimate standard, all things should be connected to God.

We see children playing on the streets, running about, laughing and shouting. They look so happy, so innocent when compared to adults. But still they are born of stained lineage, of a heritage of sin. (Romans 3:23) And if innocent children are in such a condition, what can we say about adults? Our source of happiness must be in God, but we are alienated from God and live in sadness and misery. We should think and act in connection with God's will, but the opposite is true. We are living this way as individuals and as families. And those individuals and families form the world.

This kind of world is not pleasing to God. If God exists, He is sad about this situation and would want us to live in an ideal world. In fact, we can be sure He will make one for us. But the whole population of the world is separated from Him, so in restoring the world into an ideal one, He cannot do it all at once, but only little by little. He wants to work on the individual base, trying to locate a person who is entitled to such a world. He will then restore a family, a nation, and at last a whole world beginning with that one individual who can meet God's standard. First of all God must locate one person, one single man, a central figure. Finally this one person will be known and influential in the whole world. The project is not a simple one; it may take many years. God needs time to develop His providence. He works gradually, restoring people one by one and family by family. When He restores one person, it may appear that He's working with that man alone. Or we may think that God is interested in just one particular family or nation.

Sincere Christians today pray earnestly and strive to lead a life of faith in order to insure their own salvation. That has required the full effort of Christians. Once their own salvation is secure, then Christians try to save their families. We are accustomed to doing that much, but not far beyond that. We did not realize that if we really struggled to win our nation under God's will, our families and ourselves would be included in the scope of that salvation. By setting our goal at a higher standard and pursuing a broader scope, lesser levels would be already included as saved. Today Christianity is declining in the world, and this is the cause. Christians have not restored nations as the solid foundation on which God can work. Again, Christians today expect that when the Lord returns, he is coming to save individual Christians. But when the Lord comes again, he will establish a whole nation of faith and restore the entire world.

In the days of Jesus Christ people had the same expectations. Many religious people of that time thought that God had prepared 4000 years of history to send Jesus to the Jewish people in order to save Israel. They expected and desired that when the Messiah came, he would take revenge on their enemy nations. According to their interpretations of prophecies, they believed they would be the leading nation of the world and all others would come to their knees before them. They never dreamed that when the Messiah came he would want them to sacrifice themselves and their nation for the sake of the world. If they had believed that, Jesus could never have been crucified.

If you were in God's position, would you prefer to save one nation or just one individual -- or the whole world? The answer is clear. God wants to save the whole world. Now, are Christians thinking that way today? If not, is there any other religion which is seeking to save the whole world? There may be religions whose goal is to win the world, but in that case they want to subjugate other religions and have all other people come under that religion. But there is no existing religion which intends to save the world at the cost of itself or at the sacrifice of the people of that religion.

As you know, even in the Communist world, the ideal is to unite the whole world into one, which is to be the happiest world for people to live in. But we have seen the fact that in the Communist world itself there is a rupture between Soviet Russia and Red China. If it is impossible for them to be united into one within their bloc, it will also be impossible for them to form one world under their ideology. Even though Communism as an ideology advocates the unity of all people and making the whole world into one, Communist nations cannot put the ideology into practice. To really bring about world unity, it is necessary to respect the value of the view of other people, but in this case each country wants to dominate the other. That is how the conflict came about. Russia dreams of the sovereignty of her people over others, for example; but in order for them to make Communism a worldwide ideology, the Soviets must be ready to sacrifice their own people for the sake of the whole world. That is why it will be impossible for them to bring the whole world under their ideology. If the Communist people had been ready to sacrifice themselves in order to make their ideology a worldwide one, transcending the tribal and then the national levels, they would not have failed.

In the democratic world, also, there are difficulties. The United States has so far been the leading nation of the world, working to equalize the conditions all over the world by aid to other countries. But since she is withdrawing from parts of the world for fear of being herself weakened, other countries are not quite carrying out their missions. The founding ideology of the United States was Christianity. If the people of the United States would put themselves in the position of Jesus, and pray to God, "Let the whole world be saved, even if our nation may have to be sacrificed," the United States would continue to be a great nation. Then this nation, even though it might be faced with disaster, could be resurrected as Jesus was, and would be able to save the whole world.

Recently we have seen the policy-makers in America thinking of the benefit of this country alone and having nothing to do with the outside world. They wouldn't seem to mind if other nations perished. The United States has been the one in history until now to stand in the forefront in terms of trying to save the other nations from corruption and danger. But since the United States is withdrawing from that position, we can see no other nation taking that place. If there is a God at all, He would look for a nation, even if a small one, in which the people would be ready to save the whole world at the sacrifice of themselves. If the people of any nation were armed with that kind of ambition, that nation would become the leading nation. God has got to make that out of them. But is there any such nation existing in the world today? No.

In the process of creation, God poured out all His being into the universe He made. That is to say, He sacrificed Himself in creating. In the course of restoration providence, also, those in the position of the subject must be ready to pour out all their being to those in the object position. So to save our families, nations, and the world, we must be willing to sacrifice ourselves, our families, and anything we have. We may reach the conclusion that the Kingdom of God on earth can only be brought about by that kind of attitude, not by the desire to bring all other people under our own sovereignty.

You must be ready to love your family more than yourself, love your relatives more than your family, love your nation more than your relatives, and love the world more than your own nation. It may be easy for individuals to sacrifice themselves for their families. Each family member may be ready to sacrifice for other members of the family. Among families it may not be too difficult, because good families would be ready to do that for others. But between nations it will be very difficult. Toward neighboring nations you may have a good feeling, and you would be willing to give up to some extent your own for the sake of that other nation. But beyond that point, when there are great differences in customs, traditions, and history, it may be difficult for you to want to sacrifice your nation for those other nations.

There is no religion which teaches sacrificial spirit today of the quality which can embrace the world. If this kind of life cannot be lived by human beings, God has no hope to be able to restore the world, because He cannot change the world by Himself. God must work through man. If no one is ready for that task, God cannot save the world. But wherever God could find such a person, such a family, such a nation, such a religion, He would be very pleased, and He would work through those people and that religion.

We must be ready to sacrifice our nation in order to save the world. We must be willing to sacrifice our families to save our nation and the world. And we must sacrifice our own selves to save our families.

When you have won victory on the individual level, when you have saved yourself by bringing your body to obey your heart centered on God, then what will you do? You must reach the level of sacrificing yourself for the world by working through your family and your nation and leading them to live the same way. You are inclined to think that after you have perfected yourself, you are going to be the boss in your family. But you are forgetting that you are living with the purpose of saving the whole world. Even your family has that purpose; it does not exist just for yourself. Then what would you do to make your family a success in God's sight? It is not enough that husband and wife love each other. In loving each other you must be doing that for the salvation of the nation and for the salvation of the world. In order for you to be able to save the whole world you must know that you must be able to sacrifice your nation, and your family for the nation.

We are taught that we have to make an offering to reach God. That means that what we are going to save at the cost of the offering is greater than the thing we are going to sacrifice. When you are going to save your family at the cost of yourself, you have already obtained something greater – your family. And when you are going to save your nation at the sacrifice of your family, you will have gained the nation, which is greater than your family.

When you make an offering before God, would you offer Him leftovers? You would choose the best thing out of what you have and would want to give Him that. What you cherish most will be your offering. When Noah spent 120 years of the prime of his life in the business of building the ark, he was offering the best part of his life to God. Abraham was in the position to have to offer his wife to God, then even his beloved and only child. For him it was more difficult than to sacrifice his own self when he had to offer his son. Moses experienced the same course. When he was going to receive the Law, he fasted for forty days and went through many difficulties and hardships. He was ready to sacrifice himself, his own life, in making the offering before God.

The same is true with God. He would ask us to make offerings, but on His part too, He has to give something for the salvation of man. He has to sacrifice the man who makes the offering. That means God barely has won that precious person Himself, and already He has to sacrifice him. We know that after choosing and preparing a nation to receive the Messiah, God was ready to sacrifice that nation for the sake of the world. People, however, did not realize that fact. They thought that the Lord would come to save their nation and put it above all other nations and that God would help them to have that position.

What is God's desire and our desire? That is to restore the nation which God can claim to be His. In order for us to be able to do that, we must eliminate the evil condition. At all costs, even at the expense of ourselves, we must establish the kingdom of God on earth. We are living for that purpose. The whole earth will be our country. In God's sight there are no national boundaries. We have to unify the whole world under God's will. With all nations put together, they will be one people in God. With all those people in cooperation with each other, we are going to build God's kingdom on earth.

To do that is your mission as well as mine.

You are just individual people, but you must be proud of being representatives of all the people of the world as citizens of the kingdom of God on earth. You must have that ideal, that thought, each one of you. Above all the worldly sovereignties, God's must be the ultimate one.

If Adam had not fallen, the family multiplied from him would be the world. He would have played the role of the first ancestor of the citizens of God's kingdom on earth.

In the course of restoration, every one of you must be thinking of yourselves as a starting point. You are going to be blessed in marriage and give birth to your children, and you will be the true ancestors to your descendants. From then on all will be citizens of the kingdom of God. Christ comes again inheriting God's sovereignty, and with him as the core, you must be able to spread that blessing out, establishing the kingdom of God on earth. The whole earth being our land, the whole population of the earth being our people, God's sovereignty will reign over all mankind.

You must strongly believe that you women are the representatives of all women on earth, and you must put yourselves in the position of mothers to the descendants of the people of the world. With true faith, men are the representatives of all the men of the earth. The whole earth will be God's, the whole population of the earth will be citizens of God's kingdom, and the sovereignty of this world will be God's sovereignty. We must pray for that day and fight for it with gratefulness.

We have the glorious kingdom as our mission directly ahead of us. We are going to sacrifice ourselves for that cause, and we are destined to become the joyous citizens dwelling in the love of God. And for that cause let us march on.

Challenge and Victory

We are both men and women here. The path of life for women is obviously different from that for men. What women feel is different from what men feel. Within the life of any individual, there is a difference between his childhood, youth, middle age and old age. Not only in human life is this true, but also in nature. We see four seasons coming one right after the other. If you were to insist that you would always live in summer, and if you never prepared for the winter, you would have a problem when winter arrived. In the winter, those who don't think of the coming spring and confine themselves in snug, warm rooms will be uncomfortable in the spring. Can you insist on wearing winter clothes when summer comes? No, you need to change your clothes to suit the season.

This is exactly how it happens in our lives. Those who belong to the summer of life – which is the prime of youth – want to have eternal youth. But that is not possible. It's natural that there must be change. But are you not inclined to insist on remaining the same age? You are afraid that by changing, you will somehow decline. You know from experience that you don't always go up. Every day your mood has ups and downs. After having passed through the day, if you find that you have had more ups than downs, then you can safely say that you have had a good day. If you have had more downs in a day, you will say that you have had a bad day. You may think that you want to have no downs at all in your life, but that cannot be.

In the world of change, how to digest what we encounter and make it something good is always the question. More than anyone else, young people are faced with constant changes, because their dispositions are like that. You seek stimulating things, and you want to have variety all the time. If you can digest the problems and changes and still want to have more, that's all right. But if you don't have this digestive power and yet desire to experience new things every moment, that's not possible. You as young people must learn to manage your own problems. You do not know the future before you, so you need to learn how to go through the path of life in such a way that you will be able to think of every event positively, so that you can continually grow.

If you say you hate to undergo disciplined training because you don't like it, or that you just can't stand it, you have been defeated already. You must have the attitude that you want to face whatever comes with great expectation and interest. You must not look through just one point of focus, but look around at your situation in all four directions. Looking at the Hudson River, you know the deep water runs silently. But upstream there have already been many events: sometimes the water swirls in a deep eddy; sometimes it pounds down on the rocks, as in the waterfall; sometimes it rushes past big rocks or runs over small pebbles to be gathered into the ocean. As you may have seen in the movies, if you are faced with a very rough current when in a boat, you cannot just look immediately in front of you, but you must set your gaze far and wide, and you must be quick to manipulate the boat. Otherwise it will be wrecked on the rocks right before you. In your life, too, there are waterfalls; sometimes the water will even form walls or cliffs in front of you. So you must dodge quickly past one place or steer directly through the waves in another.

You must be prepared for the wave. If you are riding the wave, however hard you may struggle not to be carried on the current, you cannot resist it. If your destiny is to float on the current of the Hudson River, you must flow as it does. You may very possibly be like the waterfall or the water running past the rapids, but you must not become discouraged by the roughness of your course. If you are trained on this course, things to come will become easier for you to handle. If you take interest in what you are going through, and if you are thrilled to find new adventures, then when you are faced with even greater difficulties, you can tackle those with more zeal and capability. But if you are unwilling to confront the problems occurring around you and are afraid of them, then you will not be able to turn the experience into training to face new problems. Only by having gone over the rocks and waterfalls can you lead yourself to the heart of the ocean.

There are many ways of life: the life of an ordinary man, the life of a sacred man, and the life of a great leader. When you are asked which one you want to become, all of you, I am sure, will answer, "I want to become a great leader." But a leader cannot be made overnight. Such a person has to endure many trials, and with often desperate effort he must persevere and be ready to face still more.

Those who have been faced with life-and-death situations – not once, but continuously – know how to give themselves in everyday life. Suppose there is a great general. Looking into his past, we find records which show that he fought in many battles, was sometimes defeated and sometimes victorious. As many experiences as possible would be important to his record. But if that general in time of peace would not be willing to live sacrificially for his nation, his fame would quickly fade away. His attitude must be that of a patriot; he must always be ready to give his life in the face of need.

We must look at how the water runs down from the mountaintop. It will encounter many obstacles. If we compare our lives to that stream of water, where are we? When we look at the world as a whole, the world situation is somewhere in mid-course – not quite reaching the deep ocean. Before its coming to the ocean, the world may one day be at Niagara Falls. Can the drops of water say, "I hate to pound down the cliff"? At the top of the cliff, you must get ready and say to yourself, "It's thrilling, and I want to jump down from this cliff and reach the ocean as soon as possible." If you are eager, then you will succeed and attain your purpose. When you survive having gone over a Niagara Falls, then every other person who is faced with the waterfall will come to you. Many people may try to give the new ones advice, describing how difficult a job it is to crash over the cliff – but you with experience are the only one qualified to do so.

In the world under the Roman Empire, Christians were faced with iron bars when they tried to advance. But if Christianity had not been persecuted by Rome at that time, I don't think Christianity would have progressed to today's level. If there is only a low dam, then a strong current of water will overflow it. Because Christians had more onward determination than the stopping power of Rome, Christianity overflowed and flooded the Roman nation and the world.

When you are tired you doze off, but you yourself are not aware of that. You may try hard to resist your sleepiness, and you may mean not to fall asleep, but you do so just the same. If these two small openings for your eyes close, then all the rest of your body will come into harmonized action, and you fall asleep. Every cell of your whole body will cooperate with that one action. When you doze off, all the parts of your body do so. In order for you, one individual, to survive adversity, you must feel that the whole universe, not just your relatives and neighbors, will come to your aid. If someone pulls out one hair of your head, does that part alone feel the sting, or your whole body? Every human being is a part of the universe, so if one part fails, the whole universe will ache over that failure. If you succeed in a mission, you must not think that the success belongs to you alone. A river is the accumulation of raindrops, though out of the water some portion must evaporate.

You must want to ride the current that beats against the rock, and with that force you can go ahead, joining the mainstream until you reach the mouth of the river; then you can join the ocean. In God's providential course of restoration, there is also a mainstream. Would you join that great river, or one of the tributaries? Everyone will answer, "The mainstream." But unless you can flow past all the obstacles in the tributaries, you cannot meet the main river.

Our life itself is something like a river. You are here going through training, seated side by side; but once you are scattered and sent to your different missions, then you will be like small streams running through your own courses to reach the mainstream. Would you as a drop of water try to join other raindrops – or would you rather absorb other drops of water into yourself, to form a mainstream yourself? Even if you may have to be tributaries for a while, I want you to be the one to gather other drops of water until you join the main current.

We cannot foretell if all of us here will meet at the mouth of the river. We do not know if we all will reach the heart of the ocean. If you are faced with any power stronger than your own determination, what will you do? If you are faced with a power greater than your own strength or spirit, will you be absorbed and surrender? It is not easy to answer.

Sometimes, people are small-minded. If a difference of interest occurs between two of you, you may become angry with each other and argue. Then someone else may want to reconcile the conflict between you and say pacifying things to you both; but you will only become more fierce toward each other. If you had a broader mind and would let the other go, that person would cling to you and want to solve the problem. You should be of such a broad mind that you can smile and return to the work waiting for you. If you are like water trying to surmount a wall, you will be eager to rush over it as soon as possible and join the larger body. Time will solve the problem. If you can pass on from the difficult place quickly, you will succeed. Tell the other drops of water, "You may stay there, but I must rush on."

When you are scattered all over the country, you can write back and forth. Some will say in their letters, "Oh, I am faced with troubles, and all this is not what I expected. It's a most difficult job to witness to the people." It is very likely that those who receive letters will be influenced by that. In the life of faith, we must not fix our glance on what is happening only at the moment, but look far off into the future, toward the goal where God is hailing us. We must never be settled in one place.

As you go along, you must always be able to add something to what you are. If you pass by a village and there is a great fight taking place, you should get into it, reconcile it, and then go along your way. In that way you can help solve others' problems, and you will also pave the way for others following you.

You have seen many successful people in the history of America. In their backgrounds, they have many adventures. The more they have had to overcome in their lives, the greater people they are. If someone has had even one more such experience than another, he is a little bigger person than the man with less experience.

The harder, the more challenging the situation is, the more progress you will make. Do you realize that? You are so anxious to be successful, but if you have no zeal to fight through the way to success, you will not meet it soon. You may say that in order to go to San Francisco, you must ride in a bus, an airplane or a train. But you must have no such fixed notion. If you really want to go to San Francisco, you must be able to walk there.

When I was imprisoned in North Korea under the Communist regime, it was right in the prison cell that I learned that lesson and became resolved to fight forever against evil. I was confident that I would win over it. I said to myself, "However strong Kim Il-Sung's power may be, if I am well trained in prison and go through hardship here, I will be able to be victorious over anything." I was ready to eat any food they gave me – or even to starve. In North Korea, the winter temperature is very cold. Even though I was wearing only thin clothes without any lining, I could bear the cold. The labor in prison started at 8:00 in the morning, but as early as 4:00 they would call us out in the open air and check to see if we had anything hidden inside our clothing. Out in the cold air, people would shiver – their trembling sounded almost like thunder. In that situation, I would always say to myself, "Even if it gets colder, I will not surrender to it." I did not feel cold at all. I trained myself by giving thicker, heavier clothing to other people, and clothing myself in thin clothes. I would look for heavier work, and say to myself, "I will succeed in doing this, or I will die." With that seriousness, I fought my circumstances.

How many times did Peter answer Jesus affirmatively? It is easy to answer now. If one of your eyes is put out in battle, what will you do? If one of your limbs is cut off, what will you do? If you lose all four of your limbs on the battlefield, will you still go on? In the face of a great task, you must be ready to sacrifice everything. A raindrop beginning at the mountaintop and running down through the stream to the great river is faced with many obstacles. You must be prepared for adversity while doing great things. You must be ready to die for the cause you have undertaken, or else you are foolish to say you are following the way. If you are resolved to deny yourself and give up your very life, you will never be afraid of any difficulty. However strong the enemy's fortress may be, you will never be intimidated. You will be contemplating at least how to die a brave death. Are you like that? If you are prepared to die, you will not die, and victory will be yours. You must be resolved first of all to deny yourself.

Why do I tell you this? When our circumstances are difficult, we must be determined to face these and win over them. You must know that you are going to be defeated in the long run unless you consider your circumstances and become able to either adjust or maintain your course through everything. How to digest and conquer your environment is the question. Don't ever try to escape from life, but feel challenged and persevere on your way. On an uneven road, ups and downs are to be expected; but where there are peaks, there are valleys at another time. When you find yourself in a dungeon, you must expect that in the next moment, God will bless you with the most grace.

You must imagine yourself in a race, feeling that kind of determination. Resolve to have more strength than any enemy so that you can win over whatever the obstacle may be. I always told myself that I could eat less than other people and do more than other people, sleep less than other people and wake up earlier than others.

When you are faced with difficulties that look really hopeless, you may feel as though you are going to perish indeed; but there is always a way out if you look for one. Even in the prison cell, I would teach young people. I learned how to make fire even when I was alone on the mountainside. I know how to feed myself with wild herbs. I always imagined that I might be faced with any difficulty; then I studied to learn the secret of overcoming that. If you have vowed before God for any great cause, you have to keep your promise.

Try to focus on today, on this very moment; and if you are the victor in your heart right now, you will be victors after going through the entire course. So, you must be alert in winning the very moment you are faced with for the side of God.

Way of Life

Each of you as an individual is born and raised in the love of your parents. You go through kindergarten, primary school, high school and the university, and eventually your view of life is broadened to a wider scope. You want to see what the society is like and what the people around you are doing. You find yourself belonging to one of the many nations of the world. You will want your nation to prosper more than any other nation. You want to be successful, and you become interested in the opposite sex. You want to have a sweetheart, and you desire to get married to that person and build a home of your own. You want to give birth to your children, and in the parent's position you want to educate them as your parents have educated you. In order to raise your family you must have a job. To most people, success means to be able to make more money for the happiness of their family. In this way you grow old.

In the worldly sense, there are happy and unhappy people. Some are unhappy because they have no children, and some are unhappy because their families are being broken up. Still others are unhappy because they have been discharged from a high position or because of the bankruptcy of their company. Kings, presidents and other responsible officials in each nation feel unhappy when their country is defeated by other countries. We can well see that in the world there are people who are happy, but there are more people who are unhappy. There is not a single man in the whole world who would choose to have unhappiness or misery; everyone wants happiness. However, some things are not within our reach. We cannot always do what we would like.

In the United States people are seemingly happy and have an abundance of everything, but in their hearts there usually is unhappiness too. To a certain extent, the people of the United States have been happy and blessed, but when one experiences misery after having had happiness, one feels even more miserable. Suppose a certain couple seems very happy. Inwardly, they may be very unhappy. In homes, especially, there is often a breakdown. You may be successful in your worldly career, but that can become a failure in the next moment.

What is happiness in the true sense? In a word, happiness can be found in the position where we have things which other people do not possess. You are elevated, elated; you are happy when you can give to other people. You are happy when you can enjoy a position higher than other people's. By giving and taking with other people, you feel happy. On the other hand, if you cannot give out to others, they cannot receive, and they feel unhappy. You are happy when you can give things to other people, when you can share the position, wealth, knowledge, and whatever you have that is virtuous with other people. If you are satisfied with what you are, with the position and everything else you have, then you can call yourself "happy." If you can share love with each other, that makes you feel happiest of all.

Comparing yourself with successful people, you often ask yourself, "Can I be that way? Can I ever be that kind of person?" You find yourself limited by your knowledge, your position, your authority, and many other things; but your desire and ambition have no limit. When you have limitless desire and limited circumstances, how can you find the balance between those two? This is what gives all of us agony. Thus, we find there is only a small difference between the commoner and the prince. Everyone has to solve this problem.

There seems to be no solution. That's why people look for the key in philosophy and religion. In philosophy you search outwardly, and in religion, you look for the key inwardly, or spiritually. Motivated in this way, people have developed philosophy and religion, and today we experience the maturity of this history of search. In the external sense, in the political philosophy of democracy, freedom-loving people have grown to a certain level in their cultural tradition. On the other hand, Communism has been growing strong and opposes democratic ideology. People are struggling to find the more righteous one of the two ideologies. In the midst of struggle, the religious world is holding the mainstream of thought, and it cannot be overcome by the opposing power.

The struggle between democracy and Communism will end in two possible ways: either one of them will absorb the other, or both, exhausted, will diminish and perish and a third philosophy will arise. We are now living in the age that will see the outcome. Democracy and Communism have long struggled; they are both tired, and they are talking of detente, peaceful co-existence. They both say that their people are going to enjoy real freedom and peace, and we will all eventually be settled in the peace they proclaim. If they fail to fulfill their promises, some new ideology will arise that will deny all the "isms" and ideologies that have existed. Then everything of the past must be denied. This is because the already-established system of family, society, nation, and everything else will have been tested and proved a failure. So we will have to deny and remove all those things and change the system or tradition.

Since everything would have been tested and have failed, some people would feel free to live just as they please without any restrictions. That group is what we call "hippies." They don't want to work. They wear ragged clothing, and even inside out or backwards. They may do anything, acting as though they are the guests of society. The ordinary people around them are helpless; they cannot change these people. The society does not know how to respond. If their parents warn them against their way of life, they protest against their parents and ask, "What do you have that is better than what we have?" They demand of the older generation: "What have you done for us? The society is corrupted and you are still advocating the tradition and culture you have built, but it is rotten and decayed. What have you better than what we have?" This group can make the foundation for another group to come to deny the world and society. This happens to be the world situation today, and society cannot blame those people for protesting. Almost all of them are inclined to continue their way.

Our standards of what the family, nation and community should be are all broken down. There is only darkness, and we have no idea what direction to take or how to evaluate things. We are faced with the ruin of our view of value. In the former days we esteemed love in marriage and in the family, but now love has fallen far below the standard of past tradition. In the democratic world people say even of their leaders, "Well, he is just another man, no different from myself." Everything of virtue has been levelled. There remains no high view of life for future generations to pursue. But still we cannot abandon our human ambition and desire.

Of the two powers, shall we follow democracy and the United States, or shall we follow the Communist world and respect the Soviets and other Communist powers? Is there any religion in which we have not been disappointed? People have become disillusioned by all of these. Democracy, Communism, and even religion have failed people. They feel that now everything has been tested and all have failed. We have come at last to this point on the way of life. Now what should we do?

There is natural law ruling in human society. We cannot change our sexes. Men must remain men, and women must remain women. Their na- tures and desires are different. But what do they have in common? They have the desire to enjoy something virtuous. However far-ranging our human thought, or however varied life around the world may be, we must be set truly on one common goal. We have got to find the ultimate goal which both man and woman are headed for. If we find that goal, we will be the happiest people. People may think that happiness is something that we only wish for, but which can never be attained. Who can give us happiness? Can our nation give us happiness? Can any ideology or "ism" bring us happiness? We can only be scornful of past ideologies which promised to do so.

When you are born in a small country, you feel so limited, and you dream of coming out of that country to the United States. But when you come here, you don't find so much difference from your own nation. Even though there is tremendous wealth here, even though dreams are realized here, you are not going to be contented. You will want to go further. In the world, people are not contented with what they now enjoy. Their missions and desires are always far ahead of them. Isn't that true? That means that what we already have is not the ultimate happiness.

A boy may want to marry a girl and at one point that is the goal. After it is attained, are the two happy? No. They want to have something more. They have learned about each other, and not so much remains there now. Real happiness is something that we can never exhaust, something we can enjoy forever.

So what is the source of such happiness? Can any individual be the source of happiness? Can another person give everlasting happiness to you? After thinking about it, we can come to the conclusion that if there were no God, we would have to create one. We must have God at least in our imagina- tions. Even though we might be deceiving ourselves, if we had that God in our imaginations, and if by serving Him we felt that we were given ultimate happiness by Him, then we would be happy. Because no other human being can give us that. We have got to have God transcendent of human life, or life has no meaning. At this point, if we discover that God really does exist, how happy we must be! We should feel as if we could turn the whole world up- side down. If a group of people can really know God and work in the love of God and for the cause of God, society will be attracted to that group and will watch it and be anxious to see the group successful. We have to put this into practice, and we are happy to carry out our mission.

People of the world go to school and get married, and they seek posi- tion and status; but they are never satisfied. Here we know God is above us, leading us and working through us. So everything we do is very meaningful to us, and what we say and what we do is of higher dimension than what others are saying and doing. People generally are doing things that have limited scope. But we are doing things without limitation. We have a super-existence above us – God, our Father. So we do everything in accordance with His will. We eat and sleep for the great task which He would have us do. We always seek to act in accordance with God's will; that is our standard. We marry to bring the family, society and nation into accordance with God's will. We marry because we want to come closer to God. We do everything because we want to be near Him. We want to restore the family, the nation and the whole world because we know that by winning these things back to God, we as individuals can come closer to God. We want to go to a meeting point with God, where we can reach Him and win Him for ourselves.

In the external world, the ideologies of democracy and Communism have been struggling for so long. They are both so worn out that people don't know which one they belong to. But in the world of higher dimension, the more we struggle the more valuable the achievement. In the love of God we will enjoy everlasting happiness. So it is only too natural for us to reach the conclusion that we can attain the goal of human happiness in a higher dimension, and that it will last forever. Since learning about God we are strong and happy people. We know only too well that God is love and that we will enjoy God's love in doing everything. In going through education and enjoying even high positions and wealth, we know how to return all things to God, and we can enjoy things as having been given by God, our Father. Compared with all people we are the happiest. That's what makes us happy. We said that when people possess things other people do not, they feel happy. Since we possess things of greater value, we are happy.

In giving, too, we must not be narrow-minded; we will not draw small circles around ourselves. We must be generous people. We want to give out things not only to our family members, but to friends and neighbors and the society around us. We want to give out not only things, but our whole being to the last man alive, stretching ourselves until we can reach the other end of the world. There is no limitation according to East and West in our life. Nations which have long been enemies can come together in our movement and love each other. We can enjoy things among ourselves, sharing with each other what we have cherished. Since there is no barrier whatsoever, there are no enemies whatsoever; we can safely say that we are the happiest people. In human society some people want to possess more than other people, and they want to invade others' ownership to possess more people, more land, and so on. That's what makes people fight each other. But here there is no such thing. If you want to possess things with self-centered motive, we know you are liable to ruin.

Here we say that everything belongs to God. Only God owns everything. What we have belongs to God. We feel that we have to return everything first to God and then be given what we need by Him. In that way, we exchange what we have with God's love. We want to return to God everything we have, and in return we want to receive God's love, which is greater than anything else. Then we want to share that love with others.

Husband and wife are proud of the love between them. The man is not proud because of the build of his body, and the woman is not proud because of her femininity, but they are both proud of there being love between them. The family, as a unit, cannot be proud of its wealth or position. It can only be proud of the love of God abiding within the family. Neighbors, relatives and friends will be envious of the family that really enjoys the love of God. Such a couple says to God, "We will return everything to you: What we have is yours – our family, our children, our nation, and everything is yours. In return we want to have your love. In your love of the family, we will love our family; and in your love of the nation we will love our nation; and in your love of people of the world, we are ready to love the people of the world." What we want to do next is to return the whole cosmos, the whole spirit world, to God and receive God's infinite love. What we are doing here is for the sake of God. We eat for God's cause, we work and do things and say things all for God's sake, and to receive God's love.

In love your trials and your struggles are not painful. Suppose there is a girl who wants to marry a very handsome man, a righteous man. She could sit up the whole night embroidering something which would please her future husband. She would never feel fatigued no matter what long hours she worked. When you work for the love of God, you cannot be made to feel tired. Therefore, however hard we have to toil and labor, we are happy to do it. This is the secret to possess love. The more you labor for the person you love, the more love you will receive from him.

You are working for the accomplishment of a great task. But here in the United States, people are not calling you. You have to knock at the door, and people are still sleeping. You have to wake them up and persuade them also to work for the great cause. That is your mission. People may be reluctant to receive your message, and they may even send you away. But afterwards, when they are really awakened to the fact that they can be brought into the life of vast dimension, they will be very grateful to you. When you knock at the doors of those people, you will have brought to them the love of God. Even though you leave their house, they will have been touched and moved by what you have said. Later on, they will come to you in gratitude. You must be aware of the fact that this is our great task, and you must carry out your mission in thankfulness to God.

Love is something precious that you want to keep deep inside yourself like a secret. This secret between you and God will make you great. In giving out the love of God to other people you are sharing your love with them, and your love rather than being diminished, will be multiplied. You will be proud of what you have given. Only by giving can we receive. So we want to give out our whole being. We want to give out our family, our clan, our nation, and our whole world to God. In return He will fill our hearts with such love that can embrace the whole world and the whole cosmos. We are rich; we are the happiest people. Then, are you going to be really generous givers? In giving to others, never expect to receive anything directly in return from them. But let them return what they have received, to God. You are returning everything to God through those people, so God will be sure to return something to you. That something is His love, which is greater than anything else in the world. You will receive things of more value than those you have given out. Through the love of God you will be in the position of God's son or daughter.

Now that you have learned the way to go in life, the more you labor for the love of God, the more you can receive love from Him in abundance. When we live in God's love, we have nothing to be afraid of. If you know that you have been doing all things for the sake of God, you are not afraid of being caught in any kind of disaster, because you know that God will keep you and protect you. If you are sacrificed in carrying out your mission because of your love for God, you will be a martyr who will long be remembered in the history of the providence of God. In the Roman Empire when Christians were persecuted and martyred, they suffered for the sake of the spiritual kingdom they expected to enjoy when they died. With the thought that they wanted to go to the heavenly kingdom of God, they endured martyrdom.

But in this world we are going through all difficulties and hardships and persecutions in order to build the kingdom of God on this planet while we are still alive. Even though we may have to be martyred here, we are struggling for the love of God. We are going to be the children of God. Knowing this, you must carry out your mission with gratitude and you must return joy to God.

God's Grief

When you are asked what is the most valuable thing in the world, you will name your life. Your life is the greatest and most important thing to you. However, if you think again, isn't there something greater than life itself? Your answer would be love; it could be nothing else. No knowledge, no authority, no power – nothing is more desirable than love.

We want to live eternally – nothing less than that. But if you were asked what you would want to live with through that eternity, your answer could only be love. Life is in your possession already. If you live on through eternity, then you will have already attained your purpose or desire. But you need something else. You don't want to live without love.

There must be something corresponding in God, because He is the Creator of life. Can God enjoy His life without love? No. However omniscient or omnipotent He may be, by Himself alone He cannot enjoy happiness. He cannot be happy, He cannot have an ideal or feel joy.

Suppose you see a man dancing around and shouting out for joy. He is all by himself. There is no one else he is talking to or who is responding to him. He has no object with him. We would call this man crazy. You say you are happy because you have your parents, your husband or wife, your sweetheart. You say to someone, "I am happy because I have you with me." Any ideal, joy, happiness or anything of virtue cannot be achieved without having an object. Strictly speaking, you are not happy because a flower exists, but because you see the flower. The flower means something to you. You are not happy because there is music, but you are happy because you hear the sounds. You are not happy because smells exist, but because you can smell fragrances. You are not happy just because there is someone else beside you, but because you can see him, touch him, talk to him. You can finally say that in the world where you do not have an object to respond to you, there is no joy, no ideal, no happiness. If that is true with human beings, then the same applies to God.

God became grieved due to the human fall. What element in Him could allow that? What could respond to the fall? If you don't have a person united with you, you have nothing to lose. Without ever having met that person you cannot even say you are sad. It's only after you have lost your object where he had been before that you feel unhappiness and sadness.

Then in what position were human beings originally in relation to God that He was made so sad at the loss of them due to the fall? We can imagine that human beings were in the responsive position of object to God as the Subject. When we look through all the creation, we can find nothing greater than man; we are the masterpiece of God's creation. Looking into ourselves, we find that our bodies are full of mysteries. Even the appearance of the human being has something great and mysterious about it. God being the Lord and Absolute One, He would have chosen the one of greatest capacity in His creation to be one with Him. That must be man. If God exists, the Subject of life, then the object of His life must be man. Since God is eternal, He would not want man to be an ephemeral being. The eternal God must have wanted man to be eternal also.

We say that God created man as His object of life. But man was more than that to God – not just an object to look at, to walk with. We were created to be objects of His love. Nothing less, nothing more, nothing other than love.

After creation, God must have looked around at everything, and He saw that all the creatures were beautiful and good. When he saw the beautiful flowers blooming in the field, it must have brought joy to Him; chirping birds, flying butterflies – all these made Him happy. He could say that He was happy, all was good. It was because He loved those things. Anything you look at – the flowers or anything else – when you say, "It's cute," "It's lovely" – then you are loving that thing already. You have pet animals and love them. In America I have often witnessed people walking with pet animals and even kissing them. If you can love flowers, birds and animals, how much more should you love human beings! If you smile at the puppy, can it smile back at you? If you talk to a bird and tell him to sing with you, would he do that, could he understand you? However beautiful the flowers may be, if you want them to dance with you, would they do that? But with another person, if you want him to do something with you, he can respond to you. If you say, "Let's dance, let's sing," that person will begin to dance and sing with you.

We can see that man is the being of greatest virtue and value to God. God cannot but love man. You can be so confident as to say that without yourself God cannot be happy.

Man in the beginning had such a relationship with God. What made God sad? What took man away from the bosom of God? If there had been any enemy to God, he would have wanted to take away God's most valuable possession. Satan set his eye on what God treasured the most. He wanted to take away God's object to be his own. God has life and love itself within Him. Life is also within you; Satan could not take it away. But love is something unfixed or mutable, and that could be taken away. Life could not be taken from you because you are life itself, and you would fight against the loss of life. He could only take away something in the object position to you. Love is the thing of greatest value that had the possibility of being stolen away.

Suppose you are a husband; there is the possibility of your wife being taken away by someone else. There are two ways that she could be taken from you – either by force or with more love than you can give her. The fall of man therefore could have only come about centered on love. According to Genesis, Eve was tempted or taken away by Satan. That could have happened either by force or by more love than her spouse would have been able to give her. At that time, then, Adam and Eve must not yet have been in perfect love with each other. If that had been true, then nothing could have taken Eve away from him. First love is the strongest. Until your death you will never forget your first love. Their first love being the strongest one, nothing could have separated Adam and Eve if that love had reached maturity. In other words, then, life was present in its perfected form in the creation, but love had not yet reached its maturity.

When we are striving to come closer to God, we have to go through three points of love. There are three kinds of love: the love of parents, the love of husband and wife, and the love of children. Out of the three, what kind of love would come first? Love of parents would come before the other two. Then we can as well say that love started from parental love. We know that all love originated in God. Love began in God as the Parents, who created man out of that love. After creation man and woman would come together in the position of parents to their children. Thus there would come about parental love, marital love, and children's love in human families. Love begins from God, and then with man and woman put together, resembling God, they experience love in their marriage. Toward their children they feel parental love, while the children feel children's love toward their parents, who return their love to God.

However, due to the fall of man, love began separated from God, in an evil world dominated by Satan. And the love we enjoy has the quality of not being centered on God's love. In order to restore these loves and return to God's heart, we must experience them in reverse order. First we must bring children's love under God's dominion, then love in marriage, and finally the love of parents. When children of God marry with God's blessing, in their unity, loving God as the Subject to them, then they can restore all three loves at once.

Because of the fall we lost three loves – parental love, marital love, and children's love. In bringing them to be centered on God, we must raise all our love to a higher dimension than what we have known on earth up to now. We can raise love above the level of Satan's dominion and back to the original standard and value of love, to the standard that matches God's love. We will find the standard of love in man as the children of God in the perfect love of God, as the married couple in the perfect love of God, and as the parents in the perfect love of God. Out of the world of Satan's control, God must find at least one such person as His child and raise him through these positions, finally bringing him to the standard of parental love. That person can be the core of God's love. The first man who wins this course of love can be called the Messiah. In him you will find the true qualities of love as the Son of God, as true husband, and as True Parent. (Isaiah 9:6)

All of these three loves must be revealed in one person because all were lost at once through Adam's fall. God is to restore these three types of love in the man He has found as His son. By having this person restore all three human loves, God can begin to restore all other people of the world as His children.

People are alienated from the love of God, but if and when they have a deep desire to love God or to be loved by Him, God's love has magnetic power. That person will inevitably be drawn to God and join the mainstream of the flow of His love. Love is the only element that can draw us to God, and the path of love alone can lead us to reach God.

Your parents, your spouse and yourself, with your children, make three levels in one family. God is the origin, you and your spouse represent the present world, and your children represent the future. So you must be able to become one at least with your own parents and children. Only love can unite those three generations of people. Only when you can enjoy those three levels of love can you say you are really happy. There will never be unhappy people in that kind of family. If you and your husband or wife are one like this centered on God's love, you can never be separated from each other. There will be no divorce there, and no quarrelling.

You are in a position to inherit the tradition formed by your parents.

Anyone who mistreats his parents or the older generation, will suffer. You must love children as God would love them. In the home, the young couple must love their parents and exemplify this to their children. If you fail to educate your children properly, your home will be broken.

Our heart of love, centered on God's love, must be enlarged and elaborated to reach out to the whole world. That is our way of advancement and how we are walking our road of faith. You as the central figure must love your spouse as God would have you do – as God would love him or her; and in loving your parents, you must be loving them as God would love them; and in loving your children, you must be loving them as God would love them. If you do that, your children will do the same toward you and their grandparents, and the parents will love you and your grandchildren in the same way. That is the measure of love, that is the true tradition of love.

By loving each other alone, a couple are not entitled to enter the kingdom of God. When they love their parents as dearly as they would love God, then they are entitled to the kingdom. And when the couple raise their children, they must not think that the children belong to them alone, but that they are God's children. The parents are responsible to raise them and educate them as God's children. If you love your children in that way your whole family may enter God's kingdom.

If there is any family receiving God's love perfectly, with God's love abiding in the family, that family can be the core of the whole world. In the Providence of God, not Noah alone, but Noah's entire family would count. God was interested in Abraham's family, Moses' family, Jesus' family – not just individuals alone.

Up to the present time, people have been inclined to think religious life belonged to some airy plane far above human life, and imagined that God would just sweep them away to heaven with His power. But the way to heaven is to broaden the scope of our love by loving the people in our homes, by loving our neighbors, by loving our friends, relatives, clans, nations, and the whole population of the world. God would take delight in living in the home where that kind of love is lived. But He would want to expand that home to ever-broader levels until the whole of mankind could become one huge family under God as our Parent. Wherever you see men of your own age, you must be thinking of them as your brothers. When you meet women older than you, you must think that they are your aunts or your mother. And toward elderly women, you should feel as though they were your grandmothers. The outgrowth of that kind of heart will be one family over all the world.

We have been talking about how to restore big things – the family, nation, and world – but the core of everything is to restore yourself into God's full love. You must establish and build the three levels of love in yourself by deeply living your life. Unless you give birth to your own children, you don't realize fully the love of God in you. Anything in the world can be understood only by our own experience of it. In restoring yourself, you can realize the true love of God in yourself. Then through love in your marriage love is broadened or elevated to the next level. When you are a parent to your children, your love is still more elevated, and reaches a greater dimension.

You must be very eager to find those experiences and restore them in yourself. You must be able to really feel God as your loving Parent, abiding in you, illuminating you. To feel that, your mind and your body must be united into harmonious oneness. Only then can you be loved by God. If you are experiencing God's love to that degree, you will be full of gratitude and feel even intoxicated in God's love. Even Adam and Eve did not experience such love; if they had they could never have fallen away from God.

As individuals, our desire is first to experience God's love personally. Any man who becomes fully one with God in love would think, "I am the happiest man in the world. I am loved by God in the true sense." Any woman receiving that fullness of love would feel she is the happiest woman in the world. When that man and woman reached maturity, God would be happy to bless them in marriage, and there they could experience the love of God on a higher level. By their being put together, they would feel the whole world is united into one around them. With the whole creation around them, protecting them and giving them joy, they would feel love surrounding them – love coming from God above them, and love coming from their children below them.

In the Western world, people often marry without their parents' consent. But that is not according to God's standard. More than anything else, you must think that marriage is for your descendants. Think back. You are born out of the lineage of your forefathers. You don't belong to yourself. You were not initiated by you. Love itself is the source of lineage. Love being more than your life, your lineage must be more to you than your life. You will love your family more than your own life. Matrimony passes on the tradition of your love to your descendants. When you leave the earth, your children and grandchildren and all of their children will be left behind you, seen by other people, even though your love is not visible. Love cannot be seen; it dwells invisibly within you and works through you. But when you find a husband or wife with God's love, together with that person you can create children, making your love concrete in them.

In loving your spouse, you are transcendent of your two lineages. When you love your husband or wife, remember that that person is the fruit of past generations and the starting point of future generations. You must put such vast value in your husband or wife.

Love is something you inherit from your forefathers. In the West, you are blessed in marriage by a minister or sometimes by a person of high rank, such as a judge. But ideally your parents bless you in marriage, just as God would have blessed His children, Adam and Eve, when they reached maturity. In that case, the parents would bless their children, saying, "You are my life, you are my love, you are my everything. I am so happy that you have reached maturity. I am now blessing you to be man and wife. I want you to love each other as we, your parents, have done. Become one with each other, resembling us, and give birth to wholesome children, multiplying your future generations forever." In that situation you would long to be like your father and long to be like your mother and long to have the love that they had. Such an event can only be imagined in a world centered on God's love.

As children to your parents, you would never want to see your parents separated. You would want to have harmony in the family. Would you like to fight your parents? Never! Then, where does the harmonious tradition begin? From your parents, from your grandparents, their parents, and their parents. And they inherited that tradition from God ultimately. Children's love, marital love, and parents' love must be put together in one in you. You must always have three levels of love in yourself.

Of the three kinds of love, which one is central? Which is closer to God? Parental love. If you have your grandparents, you must really be able to love those elderly people as you would God. Age-wise, you must unite the three loves within your own heart — love for the old, love for the middle-aged, and love for the young. You must be able to experience those three types of love. If your grandparents are dying, both your parents and yourself must be in the same degree of grief and sadness. If your parents were to pass away first, both your grandparents and yourself must feel the same grief about that. In a situation where there is joy, too, if one of the three has joy, the other two will be equally joyful. In your family, all will be one in heart.

Where does God's grief begin? In the path of true love, on the way of heart, either happiness or grief will be found. Everything starts from love. When love is created, there is happiness. But when the loving heart is lost or wounded, there is grief. The loss of love made God grieve; nothing else could have made Him sad. He did not want wealth, position, knowledge, or any such thing. He wanted love, and He wanted also to exercise love. If God can find love in you, find in you His love, God will be happy. But if He cannot find the love of God in you, He will be saddened. He will be saddened if He cannot find His love in couples and if He cannot find the love of God in parents. How much do you want to have God's love? You must be a dynamic, responsive object to Him, so that His love may explode within you.

Have you ever experienced such love? Have you ever been so happy in the love of God that you had almost to weep from that love? But that's not enough; you must experience that degree of love in all three kinds of love. The love of God must be so powerful as to connect God, mankind and creation and bring them into absolute harmony and oneness. Love must flow from one to the other.

God is grieved over the fact that man lost His love. In order to reach you, God has gone through the whole course of the history of restoration, struggling through the long years to regain true love. So from your part, you must not stay idle. You must work for the sake of God and the world, rushing to meet Him from your side. If you fight against Satan and win over his power spiritually and physically, you will stand in the position where no evil power can ever invade you. You will become perfectly one with God. There you will meet Him, and you will find that He has been at that point all along, waiting for you and looking for you.

Where is the point where you can meet God – in your room, or on the front-line of the world? On the front-line. Then are you going to enter the struggles of the world reluctantly and tearfully, or willingly? Our desire is the unity of our minds with God, our bodies with our minds, and our whole being with other people. Only by achieving that unity can we restore ourselves on the individual, family, national and worldwide levels. We must come to the position where we long for God very, very much. When we miss any other individual, any family, any nation, or the whole ideal world, very much – then to that extent and to that degree God will be there waiting for us. And we will meet Him when we have found those things we are longing for. Then will you not go that way?

More than anything else, God has been sad because there has been no one who knew His heart in this way. There has been no one who knew the world that God wanted to restore and who was willing to fight and endure all trials and difficulties in order to meet Him in that world. Since you know these things, you have the responsibility to win the whole world and bring all things back to God's bosom. Only in that way can we realize His long-cherished hope of unity among God, man, and every true element.

God sets His hope in us, and we also have our own hopes, flickering like fires within us. But we have to multiply that fire and multiply our love to destroy the whole world of evil. We may now have only a flickering candle-light, but we want to shed light into the whole world. The light will be multiplied, and the whole world will be illuminated by it in God's love. We are the soldiers for that cause, and we are eager to liberate God from His grief.

We must not ask God to help us, but we must be willing to relieve God's agony. As Christians, we can restore God's heart through our prayer. He is praying for us. He is praying for sons and daughters to end His suffering and the suffering of the world. Can you ever pray to such a God to give you a blessing, to help you? Since we have begun from so far away from God,we can relieve God's heart little by little, as we walk the course of restoration step by step. When we walk through difficult ways, we must always pray to God, "As I taste this difficulty, I know this much more of your heart. As I go through all these things, I understand the more what you have experienced." In that way you can always have the courage and zeal to continue.

Since you know all these things, you must be doing everything for the sake of God. When you read, feel that you are reading to dissolve God's sorrow. When you sing, when you recite poetry, when you write literature, when you do anything, you must realize that you are doing that in order to make God happy. We must be different from Adam and Eve; we must be different from all people of the past. We must become such people that God can say to us, "Because of you I am so relieved. Because of you I have found again my joy, my smile, my son, my everything." If you are such a person to God, He will want to talk with you, to confide things to you. And God would want to bestow everything He has on you.

If you can relieve God's agony, if you can make God happy at last, then there is no more that can be expected of you. You can enjoy everything of virtue. Then you will have restored yourself, your family, your nation, and the whole world back to God. By doing this, we can liberate God from His grief. You can do this yourself.

If you should shed tears, sweat and blood for the sake of the whole world, you will find God has been shedding tears, sweat and blood for you.

289.96
M8185MASON 12
e.1

128059

RESEARCH CENTER
LINCOLN CHRISTIAN UNIVERSITY

3 4711 00218 7047